Praise for Michael Perry
and *Population: 485*

"Swells with unadorned heroism. He's the real thing."—*USA Today*

"In the best tradition of books that pay quiet homage to community service, place, and the men and women who live there. A perfectly pitched celebration of small-town life." —*Kirkus Reviews*

"This is a quietly devastating book—intimate and disarming and lovely." —Adrienne Miller, *Esquire*

"I have been waiting for thirty years for a fresh and talented voice to rise out of the volunteer fire service in America, and finally it has arrived in Michael Perry's *Population 485*. Perry is a firefighter/EMT and he makes you feel you are responding right along with him . . . his hard work is told with the thoughtfulness and gracefulness of a first responder who cares about people, his town, our country, and the world we live in. Firefighters and EMTs will be talking about this book for a long time to come. And, so will all readers who have a love for American literature. This is a small-town story in the big tradition of Sherwood Anderson and James Agee."

—Dennis Smith, author of *Report from Ground Zero*

"My heart goes out to anybody who knows—and writes as well as Michael Perry does—about rural small-town life. His book is often funny, sometimes heartbreaking, but always full of life, characters, and the tangled web of small-town history, daily drama, and strain of occasional weirdness that makes country living such a challenge and an adventure. If there's one thing I admire more than a man who can go home again, and does, and happily, it's a volunteer firefighter. He has written a joy of a book, as gnarly, stubborn, courageous, and full of eccentricity in all its forms as country life itself." —Michael Korda, author of *Country Matters*

"Minnesota has Garrison Keillor. . . . Neighboring Wisconsin has Michael Perry. If you read one nonfiction title this autumn, make it this one. It's that good." —*The Sunday Oklahoman*

"Part portrait of a place, part rescue manual, part rumination of life and death, *Population: 485* is a beautiful meditation on the things that matter." —*Seattle Times*

"*Population: 485* is bound to be one of the best nonfiction books of the year. . . . Filled with moments of tenderness, humor, and just plain goofiness as it takes us into the lives and homes of the inhabitants of one small town. . . . Makes for riveting reading." —*Fort Lauderdale Sun-Sentinel*

"Finely crafted, hard-to-come-by honesty." —*Hope* magazine

"With self-effacing humor, stellar wit, and phenomenal writing, Perry gives an intelligent, articulate voice to smalltowners. . . . Powerful, engaging, and often hilarious." —*The Phantom Tollbooth*

"Somewhere between Garrison Keillor's idyllic-sweet *Lake Wobegon* and the narrow-mindedness of Sinclair Lewis's *Main Street* lies the reality of small-town life. This is where Michael Perry lives." —*St. Paul Pioneer Press*

"May simply be the best book about small-town life ever written." —*Wisconsin State Journal*

"Humorous, poignant."   —*Chicago Tribune*

"A remarkable new book, sometimes comic—sometimes sad."

—*Los Angeles Times*

"Michael Perry is like a sensitive, new-age Hemingway."

—*Salon.com*

"Mike Perry's writing is fresh, witty, and rich in quirky detail. He creates characters worth remembering, takes you on journeys you'll not easily forget."

—Jeanne Marie Laskas,
author of *The Balloon Lady and Other People I Know*

"When Robert Frost wrote of the need to be 'versed in country things,' he probably wasn't thinking of traveling butchers or truck-driving singers or giant plastic Big Boys or epidemics of obesity or the big, ugly house on a hill. Then again, he never met Mike Perry. Rural America is changing fast, and Perry is one of the funniest, most astute chroniclers of those changes."

—John Hildebrand, author of *Mapping the Farm*

"This is writing which frequently evokes small-town life, and yet mercifully avoids sentimentality or treacle."

—Gayle Pemberton, author of
The Hottest Water in Chicago:
On Family, Race, Time, and American Culture

"Michael Perry's essays and humor never fail to generate listener comments. I always look forward to recording his material for broadcast, and am pleased and proud to offer his work to my audience."

—Eric Wheeler, Producer/Host, Spectrum West
(Wisconsin Public Radio)

"Hop up on the old truck seat next to Mike Perry as he racks up the miles. . . . His perceptive, witty, unpretentious writing shows a respect for his fellow travelers, whether he's riding with kids to a Christmas event or bouncing down the road toward home."

—Marcy Tveidt, Minnesota Public Radio

"Michael Perry exults in the power and elasticity of language. But not just of language, of the human spirit as well. . . . Perry's unerring, if bemused, eye paints all people as if their lives were epiphanies, which of course they are."

—Bill Friskics-Warren, *The Nashville Scene*

"Michael Perry's commentaries . . . are fun, smart, clear, and filled with good sense. Writing like this is hard to do. Perry makes it look easy."—Dinty W. Moore, author of *The Accidental Buddhist*

"The best writers take us in tow to experience fully what their subjects experience and then ask, What do we make of this? Michael Perry is such a writer . . . he guides us to confront meaning in seemingly mundane things. And, often, just to laugh, clap our hands and surrender to mystery altogether."

—Bill Hudgins, *Road King* magazine

"Language dances across Perry's pages, the clarity of poetry swinging one last time with the tough love practiced by those devoted to a dying art."   —Grant Alden, author of *No Depression*

J. Shimon & J. Lindemann, Photographers

About the Author

MICHAEL PERRY was raised on a small farm in north-western Wisconsin, where he remains a resident today. His work has appeared in numerous publications, including *Esquire*, *The New York Times Magazine*, Salon.com, *Utne Reader*, and *Cowboy Magazine*. A registered nurse by training, Perry has been an active emergency medical technician since 1988 and a volunteer firefighter since 1995. He serves on a volunteer basis with two rural rescue services and one fire department. He is the author of the critically acclaimed and bestselling memoir *Population: 485: Meeting Your Neighbors One Siren at a Time*. While his writing reflects a wide range of experience, he is proud to say that he can still run a pitchfork and milk a cow in the dark.

Off

Main

Street

Barnstormers, Prophets,
and Gatemouth's Gator

ESSAYS

Michael Perry

PERENNIAL
An Imprint of HarperCollins*Publishers*

HarperCollins books may be purchased for educational, business, or sales
promotional use. For information please write: Special Markets Department, HarperCollins Publishers Inc., 10 East 53rd Street, New York, NY
10022.

First Perennial edition published 2005.

Library of Congress Cataloging-in-Publication Data
Perry, Michael.
    Off Main Street : barnstormers, prophets, and gatemouth's gator :
essays / by Michael Perry.—1st Perennial ed.
        p.   cm.
    ISBN 0-06-075550-4 (trade pbk.)
        1. United States—Description and travel—Anecdotes.
    2. United States—Social life and customs—1971—Anecdotes.
    3. United States—Biography—Anecdotes.   4. Perry, Michael,
    1964—Travel—United States—Anecdotes.   I. Title.

E169.04P466 2005
973.92—dc22
                                                            2004051000

05   06   07   08   09   WBC/RRD   10   9   8   7   6   5   4   3   2   1

For Frank and Gene

Acknowledgments

Thanks to:

My parents—anything decent is because of them, anything else is simply not their fault.

. . . the editors who white-knuckled this collection into existence, using their red pens less to cut than to teach. Grant Alden and Peter Blackstock—for your vision of Whatever That Is, and for standing beside the scribbler when tangents were not universally loved. Matt Marion, eagerly awaiting my next infirmity. Karen Croft. Joan Fischer, Faith B. Miracle, and staff. Craig Renner and Stephen Osmond, for springing me from behind the Howard Johnson razor wire. Amy, Lane, Jon, Kim, and crew, for letting me tromp around your hopeful place despite my clunky boots. Bruce and Patti, for friendship, mentorship, editorship, and a prime fireworks spot. Hudge, for assigning a road trip that lasted for years and hatched a friendship that still rolls on—send that salad back and I'll get the check. Becky, Lisa, Michelle, Renee and Wayne, for the *Wisconsin West* start. The *Utne* crew, for revivals. Celia Meadows. Amanda Gardner and H. Emerson Blake. Rose Kernochan. Alex Heard, Brad Pearson, Ilena Silverman, Adrienne Miller, Peter Flax, Dan Ropa, Bill Foy, Liz (then) Wolf and Rina Cascone, for work not published here but essential to the trip.

. . . Frank. Editor, poet, friend, master of the wax ring. Jayne, Chris, and Mister B in memory of Audrey. The McDowell family. Racy's. John Hildebrand. Kris and Frank, for a place to type away from home. John and Julie, Germanic hipsters in the Twi-Lite. Mags, in a tuck. Wilda. ALR—friend, mentor, voice coach, spiritual advisor (*"There would never be a better time to start drinking . . ."*). Krister, for spirits in the typing machine. Lisa Bankoff, Alison Callahan, Patrick Price, Liz Piranha Farrell, Tina Dubois, Cesar Garza, Jen Hart and crew (coast-to-coast) and the man who got me pulled over by the Iowa State Patrol on I-80 for crossing the fog line while talking on my cell phone, Tim Brazier. Thank you, Scranton, from phones to forklifts.

. . . Uncle Stan and Grandpa Pete, for teaching me about the road via Mack and Greyhound. Alex, for memorizing semi logos. Theater friends, musician friends, poetry reading friends, cycle racing friends, "Nobbern" friends and neighbors. People all along the road and at readings who share a smile, a handshake, and a kind word.

Acknowledgments

Even after all that, I walk to the next room, look at the stacks of boxes representing fifteen years of typing and apologize for leaving scads of good turns unremarked. If I missed you, swing on by, but do announce yourself . . .

And come to think of it, thanks to Miss Grant. She taught me how to type.

Contents

Contents

Introduction

I am a stranger in a strange town, and the man standing beside me has just removed his pants. There are mitigating factors—he is well-kempt, we are in a Laundromat, and as a registered nurse I have seen this sort of thing before—but they fail to completely dissipate the tension inherent in sharing close quarters with a pantless stranger. I am in Seattle, on Day Seven of a paperback book tour that will have me on the road for twenty-nine of thirty-one days in October. There will be more road time in November. For the hardcover tour I mostly drove—as far north as Duluth, Minnesota, as far south as Jackson, Mississippi. I put seven thousand miles on my Chevy. Checked into the Motel 6 so often that Tom Bodett owes me a house payment. A freelance writer should know how to spell and type, but one is equally served by a certain shiftlessness and an affection for truck stops. I have been schooled by truckers and country music roadies over the years, and it is paying off. "The secret to getting somewhere isn't to drive fast," a trucker once told me. "The secret is to keep that driver's-side door shut." When I drove, I had room in the trunk for clothes. On this the paperback tour, I am traveling light. Carry-on only. One week down, and laundry has become a matter of civic obligation. And so I have lugged my laptop and dirty socks some twenty blocks to this Laundromat, where I'm typing against deadline while waiting on Dryer #11. Across the table, Mr. Sans-A-Pants is reading the sports page. Packers beat the Seahawks. Beer sales in Wisconsin remain steady.

Writers sometimes report that book tours are difficult. This sort of comment is unfortunate, and will be poorly received by single mothers, strawberry pickers and astronauts. In Covington, Kentucky, I received a call from my publicist, a heroic former dancer and Canadian named Tim. It was January, and I had been on hardcover tour since the previous September. Tim was solicitous: "How are you holding up?" I had seen a weather map earlier that morning. Back home, the day dawned eleven degrees below zero. My brothers were logging. My dad was in the middle of some deep-frozen field, flaking out hay for the sheep. The turkey factory workers, having struggled stiff-fingered in the dark to get their cars started in time to make day shift on the evisceration line, would now be well into their day of repetitive-motion meat slinging. "I think I'm going to be OK," I told Tim.

It can be a little frazzling. I was sitting in the Manchester airport at 1:49 p.m. on October 20, 2003, when Democratic presidential candidate John Edwards strolled past. I caught his eye and he grinned. I thought of toothpaste and hairspray. The contrast between our respective perkiness was alarming. Here was a man on a dead run for the highest office in the land and he looked like he was striding for the riser at an Up With People concert. As opposed to me, just three weeks into a little old book tour, looking like some sleep-deprived hillbilly who took a wrong turn on his way to the tractor pull. Of course, John Edwards had someone carrying his bags, and he wasn't afflicted with a world-class internal nose zit. I realize I'm deep in self-disclosure here, but I believe the internal nose zit perfectly captures the glamour quotient of the self-propelled book tour. It appeared front and center—right at the tip of my nose—in Portland, Oregon, the morning of my first television appearance of the tour. Pulsing red schnozz notwithstanding, I went on TV makeup-free, in part because I wasn't sure how to wield the pancake dealie (the only thing worse than no makeup is amateur makeup), and in part because I followed Mrs. Oregon 2003, and she used enough product for three of us. Nice lady, but her eyebrows appeared to be derived from a palette of ninety-weight motor oil. I posted these specific observations on my Web site, and subsequently received an e-mail from the Mrs. Oregon compound. In chastened fairness I must report that: (a) the correspondent demonstrated a gracious sense of humor; and (b) while I can get by looking like a rumpled dump truck mechanic, it is the duty of Mrs. Oregon to look like Mrs. Oregon.

As the tour moved forward from Portland, the zit thrived. It was one of those subdermal terrors, the sort that doesn't resolve itself quickly. A few days later, I spoke at an emergency medical services convention banquet and my nose had achieved such a Rudolph-like immanence that several vendors who were there to sell emergency lighting systems for ambulances approached me to see if we could work out some sort of endorsement deal. People were mostly polite about it. They somehow managed to maintain eye contact and pretend they didn't notice what had become a nostril beacon. But they *did* notice. The morning after speaking at the banquet, I did a book signing. A woman at the front of the line whipped out a tube of antibiotic ointment and squirted a dollop on my index finger. "Put it on," she said. I looked at the line of about twenty-five staring people and my face flushed as red as the zit. "Go ahead!" she said. I recognized the militant mothering tone and knew resistance was futile. Dabbed a little on my nose. "The inside, too," she said. I just sat there gaping, much like all the people in line. "Go on," she said, in an *eat your peas* sort of way. And so we achieved what is so far my pinnacle book tour moment: your Correspondent, sitting in a chair before a handful of fans, finger up his hot red proboscis, swabbing bacitracin into the far reaches of his authorial nostril. Oprah, the boat has sailed, and you missed it.

The point was not to write about the book tour. The point was to convey how grateful I am for the chance to be out there at all. In 1989 I left a perfectly good career as a registered nurse in order that I might try my hand at writing. It was a half-baked decision at best. For years I wrote everything and anything: three-hundred-word pieces on call waiting for the local business newsletter; radio commercials for a used car dealer; a chapter for a medical-legal textbook about death by gunshot. My friend Al and I put together a television ad for a frozen pizza maker in which I composed and lip-synched the lyrics "*When it's time to eat-za, I like Roma pizza.*" As a freelance writer, you're never really sure where your next gig is going to come from, so you take 'em all. Like any musician playing weddings, you are working on your chops, hoping for a chance to play your own stuff. You try to balance writing for the muse with writing for the bill collector. Here and there I caught a break. The progression was spotty, the details offbeat but interminable. I'll spare you the full reprise by simply saying, from the time I published my first piece of writing until I found myself in Seattle with the Pantless Man, fourteen years passed. I spent most of those years up late, typing. But I also spent time riding shotgun in the company of sculptors, philosophers, urologists and butchers. I have been invited to cross America with truckers, sleep on country music tour buses, and sometimes, just to write about life on my own terms. Last night I was working in my little writing shack when I heard a Del Reeves trucking song on the Airline transistor. Del sang, *"I'm lookin' at the world through a windshield/ and I see everything in a little different light,"* and I thought of all the words and miles and people and helping hands since 1989, and again, I felt gratitude.

Book tours are a delight, but health insurance premiums loom, and so I keep feeding the freelance engine. Every deadline is a welcome opportunity. Thus I find myself typing in Laundromats. The selections that follow represent not a collection of *works* but of *work*, and I'm glad to have it. A man asked me recently how I deal with writer's block, and I said my muse is a bald man named Jim. He sits in a swivel chair just up the road at the Sterling Bank, and he holds my mortgage. When the words won't come, I think of Jim, and I get to typing.

And finally, thank you. I am allowed this life through the good grace of readers. There is so much shiny noise in this world, I am pleasantly flabbergasted by the idea that folks will sit still with a book on their knee. I wish you safe travels, in or out of your reading chair, and leave you with the best advice I know, given to me by a country music roadie in the middle of the night on a bus rolling somewhere: *If you see free food, eat it. If you get five minutes, sleep.*

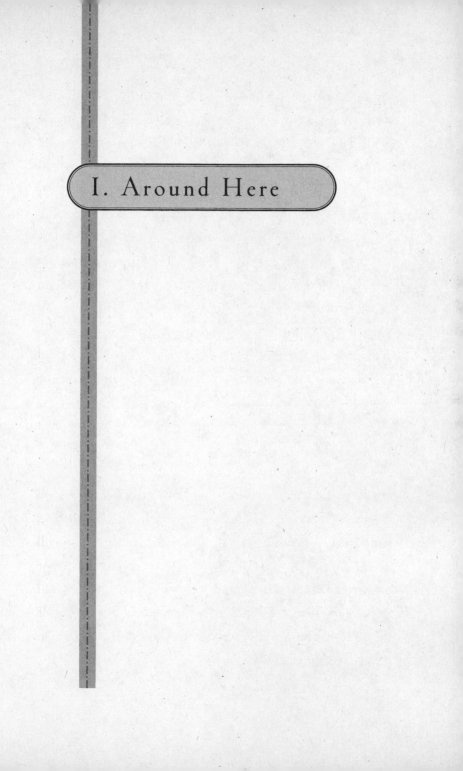

I. Around Here

A Way with Wings

One summer day when I was a child, a rocket rose through the snow in Oleander Caporelli's television, headed for the moon. I have always believed Neil Armstrong was on that rocket, bound to make his giant leap for mankind—but my little brother, who recalls the same scene, believes we saw a later mission. He was just two years old in 1969, and doubts he would remember *Apollo 11*. We do agree that we sat together on the Caporellis' floor and watched a launch, our heads tipped back as if we were tracking the ship itself into the stratosphere. The television sat on a shelf high above the fireplace mantel, the power cord clipped to a car battery. The Caporellis lived deep in the Wisconsin woods, in a small house without electricity. We had electricity on our farm, but no television, and so, with history in the air, Mom loaded us into the car and drove us down the snaking, dead-end dirt road that wound around the old cranberry bog, up a sharp hill, and then hairpinned back on itself in a long decline leading to the Caporelli place. For the last five hundred yards, the driveway ran parallel to a narrow cow pasture that doubled as a runway.

Crazy Joe Caporelli hung billboards for a living, but he had also trained fighter pilots in the Middle East. So the locals told it, anyway; or some said Korea, and others said he had been a test pilot, and you got to where you entertained all versions, because Crazy Joe had a way with wings. He carved us balsa wood jets the size of dragonflies. If you flung them low, they swooped high. Crazy Joe said the secret was in the tiny wire counterweight he crimped over the nose of each craft. Crazy Joe built a jet out there in the woods. I remember the tubular cowling on his garage floor, remember Crazy Joe with his goggles and gas welder. But when he bolted the engine to a hand-built fuselage, pointed the nose down his dandelion runway and throttled up, the jet wash incinerated the tail works. Later, he repaired the tail, switched the jet engine for a snowmobile engine, and got the rig airborne, but the Chippewa County jet age never took off.

Mostly Crazy Joe flew his homemade canvas two-seater. Summer evenings, our yard would go dark early, the sun blocked by the tall white pines sheltering the house and barn, but the sunlight that cleared the treetops gave everything to the east—the oat fields, the popple trees, the fence rows—a deep swab of color, a promise for the morning, as it were. And just when everything was glowing, there would come a buzzing from the northeast, and Crazy Joe would clear the treetops, flying through the last of the sun, his plane bright as a little red wagon against the blue sky. It was an evening ritual as common as the deer emerging in the meadows.

Some nights, after the cows were milked, and Joe had flown home, Dad took us swimming. He drove us to Fish Lake and sat on the grassy bank reading the paper. We swam and splashed until it got so dark Dad could no longer keep track of us. When he stood up, it was time to go. One day some men came to build a steel shed behind our barn. It was abominably hot, and at noon, Dad loaded the entire crew into the truck and hauled them to the lake. It was a rare treat to swim in bright sunlight. I scissor-kicked beneath the surface with my eyes wide open, trying to touch bluegills. At night, the sunfish appeared dark green, almost gray. Here at high noon, they hung in the underwater sunbeams like electrified ornaments. If you stabbed your hand out quickly, you might brush a fin before they flashed away. Given a reprieve from gravity, I hovered above the lake bed until my lungs ached for air.

Crazy Joe used to climb high in the sky over our hayfield, stall out, and then drop in a silent free fall. It put us right on the edge of our seats, waiting to hear the engine sputter and kick in. Can you imagine us, young boys in the country, playing all day, with an air show every evening? Crazy Joe used to bring his plane in low right over the garden, swoop by the house at bedroom level, dip to the clover blossoms in front of the barn, then yank back on the stick and just clear the oak trees at the end of the meadow. My brother and I would go pelting out of the house to watch. My mother had slow-motion plane crash nightmares and dreaded the day she would have to pluck Crazy Joe from the brush. Finally she forbade him to buzz the house, and he complied, but when he spotted us boys waving from the yard, he'd waggle his wings.

One night all the neighbors—from babes in arms to the two elderly Norwegian bachelor brothers who worked the farm adjacent to ours—queued up in a hayfield and Crazy Joe gave everyone rides. My brother and I rode together in the seat behind Crazy Joe, and I remember the homemade stick swaying and dipping at our knees, mirroring every move Joe made in the front. He flew to our farm and banked hard over the barnyard. He looked back and hollered over the engine noise. *"Can you see?"* My brother and I nodded. *"You can't see!"* he yelled, and flung open the side doors. We clamped hold of the seat but were transfixed. There was our yard, the green shingles on our red barn, Dad's aqua-blue wheelbarrow propped on its nose in the driveway; now we knew how it was to look down from the moon.

. . .

Today, the rockets come and go, and we barely notice. Crazy Joe disappeared in the mid-'70s, a contrail of myth drifting in his wake—how did a billboard hanger living in the woods without electricity come to possess a jet engine? My brother and I were trading Joe stories recently, and on a whim I did a nationwide phone search. Joe Caporelli came up twice. I called the first number, in rural Tennessee. Danged if Oleander didn't answer. She is sixty now, her voice thinner, but still with the flower-child lilt I remember. She was delighted to reminisce. Crazy Joe is eighty one years old, she says, and dying of cancer at home. She says she has written up an outline of all his flying stories. In fifth grade, an airplane flew over his school. He jumped out the window for a look and never returned. By age fifteen, he was building wings for Piper. In World War II, he was one of only two survivors in his squadron. She says the rumors about Korea and the Middle East aren't right, but thanks to a crash, the stories we heard about the metal plate in his head were correct.

I describe my memory of the moon shot, and she says I have the details right—even down to the silver pliers they used to adjust the antenna, but in 1969, she says, they were living in a tent, still building the house. I can no longer say I remember watching Neil Armstrong shoot for the moon. Our summers become a conflation of memories; we see them in astounding detail, like brilliant sunfish that disappear when

you try to put your finger on them. But the fascinations sur-
vive. I was a child in the country, living summers filled with
barnstormers and astronauts. The surreal was natural, and de-
sirable. Such a profound thing, the idea that one might soar.
I think of summer, and I think of flying—in the air, in the
water . . . to the moon. . . .

2001

Farther Along

If you ever watched *Hee Haw* you remember Grandpa
Jones. When he died the editors at the alternative
country music magazine *No Depression* allowed me to
compose a eulogy based on a coincidental experience. The term "alternative country" refers to a musical movement that first gained popular notice in the
1990s. In the broadest sense, the term describes
country music that eschews Nashville polish. It draws
heavily on the aesthetics of rock and the do-it-
yourself ethic of punk, and is played by people who
know Buck Owens was more than some goofball with
a red, white and blue guitar.

☐ ☐ ☐

Roughly thirty years ago, before the method-
ologies of holistic health care and the vagaries
of corporate cost cutting convened a dialectic
that produced today's burgeoning home health

care industry, my mother——then a young nurse in a small rural hospital——was recruited by the county to be on night call for a dying ninety-two-year-old woman whose family had promised to keep her out of the nursing home. The house was remotely located, and the woman's son, Henry, usually called after dark, so rather than send Mother alone, we'd pack our family of five into the Rambler, and Dad would pilot us through the swamps and backcountry to where the small wooden house sat hunched in the trees at the end of a short dirt drive. I was very young——not yet four——but I remember wolfish dogs looming through the moonlight, some tethered to brush-bound Packards, others circling the Rambler, stopping to strain at the windows.

Usually we waited with Dad in the car——uneasily, I remember——but at least once I followed Mom inside. I remember shadows, more dogs, a cousin in the corner, a disassembled engine on the kitchen table. I remember Henry ushering us in, solicitous and polite, but always with a bit of the mad scientist's assistant about him. The nursing arrangement ended in late summer, Henry's mother died shortly thereafter, and I don't recall ever seeing Henry again. For three decades the dogs and trees and old cars distilled themselves into a handful of images——a moon-soaked hillbilly gothic.

I walked up that driveway again last month, this time in full volunteer firefighter's gear. The day before, Henry, in his eighties now, had called some neighbors, said he was having trouble with his furnace. Later, someone saw smoke, and called the fire department. When they arrived, and fought their way inside, they found Henry on the floor. It looked like he might have gone back in to unchain one of his gang of dogs. Whatever the case, he lay dead, two dogs draped over his body as if to shield him from the flames. I was gone the day of the fire, but when it reignited the next day, I was part of the small crew that returned.

Oftentimes the only way to completely extinguish an extensive fire is to pull the structure apart, and so after we chopped and sprayed and sweated most of the morning, a backhoe was called in. Slowly and implacably the articulated steel arm drew and quartered the house, and as each scoop swung past, we soaked it down.

In dying, the old house gave up a lot of history. Beneath the shabby, weatherbeaten exterior, patched and teetering with trash, were signs of a grander time: a hand-turned pilaster, the remnants of a parlor. Deeper still, the original body of the house was a bulwark of hand-squared and fitted logs. And tumbling from scoop after scoop of sodden ashes, signs of something even more surprising: the skeleton of a banjo, the pleated bellows of an accordion, the shell of a mandolin, bits of a Victrola. And records. Stacks of them, thick and vintage, some melted, some expanded and separated into layers, others apparently pristine. I knew Henry had been a mechanic, knew he had mowed cemeteries, but I had never heard anything about the music.

"Oh yeah," said one of the firemen, "he gave lessons in the old days." Later that week someone stopped in the implement store where my brother works and allowed as how Henry could "play anything with strings." I looked up Henry's closest surviving relative. He told me Henry's heroes were Mac and Bob, the two blind singers who were a mainstay on WLS through 1950, and whose "When the Roses Bloom Again" was a hit in 1926. He also favored the work of Lulu Belle & Scotty, the husband-and-wife team on the WLS *National Barn Dance* from 1934 to 1958. A local man who still picks blue-grass and country gospel for church groups and nursing home residents told me how Henry taught him licks as a child: "He'd give you fundamentals, get that metronome going. He had a down-to-earth style."

Right before we rolled the hose up and headed home that afternoon, a Grandpa Jones album tumbled out atop a pile of ash and old bedsprings. Louis "Grandpa" Jones died three days later.

In 1929, at the age of sixteen, Louis Marshall Jones billed himself as "the Young Singer of Old Songs." Talk about hip—sixty years prior to alternative country, Jones was already do-ing the retro thing. At the age of twenty-two, his cohost on a morning radio show accused him of being slow and grouchy; of acting like a grandpa. The name stuck, and with the addition of high-topped boots, fake mustache, wire-rimmed spectacles and bright suspenders, so did the schtick.

Singing and frailing on his banjo, Jones worked the radio show circuit, formed a gospel quartet with Merle Travis in the '40s, and made his first appearance on the Grand Ole Opry in 1946. He had a handful of hits, and was inducted into the Country Music Hall of Fame in 1978. Most of my generation came to know him through *Hee Haw*, of course, and he remained with the show until its end in 1992.

While most performers cling to their youth, Grandpa eased into old age like he'd been waiting for it all his life. He gave his last performance at the Opry in January of 1998; he died February 19 at age eighty-four. When I heard, I thought of that album on the ash pile, and those banjo skeletons. It struck me as coincidence more than karma, but it did set me to thinking about these two lives lived over the same eight decades: Grandpa carving out a career that sustained him but didn't consume him, Henry living his idiosyncratic loner's life, refusing the company of anyone but his dogs, the indignity of his position outshone by the dignity of his choice.

Beyond the *Hee Haw* clowning, beyond the reclusive old man with his dogs and beached Packards, were two men who found joy in the same pure sounds, whose fingers could coax living history from the strings. For a few days, I despaired over Henry's lost recordings and instruments. But the more I pondered it, the more I found a kind of holiness in the idea of all that music just rising into the air, leaving nothing to be picked over by mortals. If I despair anything, I despair that for thirty years I lived within a short Rambler ride of a man who could teach mountain music, but in the end, with the old days eclipsed by noise, had no takers.

1998

Saving the Kidneys

The first thing you notice is the
momentum. The slaughter trailer resembles a
rolling derrick, all steel and cable, and as you
hurtle through the swampland in the cab of the
battered brown pickup to which it is hitched,
the trailer feels as if it is pushing more than
being pulled, its impatient weight nudging at
your back even as you try to outrun it. Mack
Most pushes the truck hard. The engine maintains a steady roar, the heavy tires growl and
whine, changing key to the tune of the road.
He brakes for corners only when it seems the
entire rumbling conglomeration must surely
launch itself deep into the bracken. The brakes
grate, the truck shudders, the turn is rounded
and the accelerator flattened once again; the
tattered brown truck flaps its wooden side

racks, gathers its resources and surges out of the curve. As soon as the speed levels off, the slaughter trailer resumes its nudging.

Most looks over. "Vacation day today!" He grins, wide open. His pale blue eyes are direct, unwavering even when they sparkle, which is often. "I'm takin' off to go to the Cities this afternoon." Later I will learn that the afternoon trip to Minneapolis is for a doctor's appointment. Most's six-year-old daughter is in chronic renal failure; her one kidney, taken from Mack's older brother, who is also a butcher, is working, but there is trouble ahead.

"Vacation day, Sunday, it don't matter. I've been on Christmas. I butchered one one hour after my daughter was born," Most chuckles, his grin undimmed. "Boss called me at the hospital. Wife wasn't too happy, but I told her, 'Hey, most guys go to the bar!' " He cocks both eyebrows, and the grin becomes knowing.

Most was fourteen when he first began work at the meat market. "I started as a cleanup boy, and worked my way up the ladder. By the time I was sixteen I was on the kill floor." He still works full-time at the shop; the traveling butcher role is a private enterprise. "The guy who started the mobile slaughter unit moved to Texas, so I took over," Most says, leaning into a curve, glancing briefly at the road ahead. Now he is on call twenty-four hours a day, ready to respond to farmers hoping to salvage a down or injured animal. Not all of his customers approach him in an emergency; a certain number of his visits are scheduled. "Some folks feel better about having their animal killed where it lived," says Most. There is no trace of irony in his voice.

Most's part-time assistant, George, sits between Most and me. Mostly he is silent. When he does speak, it is mostly in the form of colorful interjection. "Biggest animal we ever did?" says Most, "eleven-seventy-five, dressed out. White-faced steer."

George stirs. "And that's without the heart, tongue and liver."

We are at the crossroads of a small northern town, surrounded by pines. A butcher from a neighboring town is to meet us here, lead us to a farm where two hogs wait. Mack pulls into the parking lot of a shuttered drive-in diner. It is hard to imagine rolled-down windows and corn dogs this morning; as the engine dies, the heat in the cab seeps away almost audibly. It is 7:30 a.m., and the sun has been up a while, but the temperature is locked at an intractable fifteen degrees below zero.

"A warm winter, you'll see more emergency calls," says Most. He is leaning forward, tapping the wheel, looking west down the highway, impatient for the butcher. "It gets warm, they turn the cows out, then it freezes up and they slip and fall. Get a lot of broken legs, split pelvics. There he is." He twists the ignition. The butcher waves, and we pull in behind him.

The farm is far from town, a small set of isolated buildings hunkered against the cold. As we round the turn at the end of a long drive, a cat goes stock-still in mid-step, stares for a split second, then reverses itself, flashing out of sight behind a grain bin. Mack sizes up the layout, choosing an approach that will allow him access to the barn, but there is more to it. "Gotta think about how you're going to get back out," he says. "It'd be nice if all you had to do was shoot it and stick it, but y' never know. Might have to drag it around three corners."

George is grinning. "We had to hook one on the barn cleaner chain once."

"There, that'll work," says Most. "No power lines." The truck stops, the engine is switched off, and he is already gone, rifle tucked under his arm. In a clean pen, a pig grunts inquisitively as we enter the barn. The pig is on its feet when Most opens the gate, and the *whap!* of the shot is immediate. There is no talk, no prelude. The pig drops without a sound and Most is upon it, lancing the jugular with a short, swift stab. The blood rolls out, and Most moves to the next pen, where the process is repeated.

George has followed with two oversized bale hooks. He gives one to Most and the two men snag a pig each, inserting the hook through the underside of the jaw, in the same way a fisherman baits a hook with a minnow. The pigs are slid from the pen, down the manger, and into the yard. Most positions the trailer boom and grabs a knife. As he bends to the upended pig and begins to remove its forefeet, he addresses the butcher.

"Went bowlin' for the fire department last night." He circles each leg with the knife, then grasps the hoof. With a twist of his wrist, he snaps the foot free, tossing it aside. "Bowled a 256 the first game, ended up with a 591." He hasn't looked up. He slits the pig's skin down the midline from chin to groin, then runs the knife inward from each leg, angling in to the midline cut. He has stopped speaking now, pausing only to slap his flat, curved knife across the sharpener. In the wind, the metallic scraping sounds as if it is coming from a culvert.

I have ducked behind the corner of the garage, looking for relief from the gusts that sweep up through the barnyard from a bowl-like depression where the pasture unrolls to the distant wood. The morning weatherman warned of danger-ous windchills in the minus-thirty degree range. It is all that and more. I have three pens, which I rotate through my front pants pocket, deep beneath my coveralls. A fresh pen lasts for six medium-sized words. Most continues to dissect the pig. He is barehanded.

George picks up the four feet, throws them in a barrel at the front of the trailer. Pulling a knife from a bucket, he cuts out the pig's tongue. He hefts it, then it joins the feet.

Most straightens. He inserts his bloody hands in a pair of stained fluorescent-orange gloves before picking up a large, electric meat saw. "Don't wanna touch metal," he says, grin-ning again. With a quick dip of the saw, he bisects the ster-num. "Take 'er up, George!"

The winch chatters and complains, but the hog rises,

hoisted by its hocks. When it is chest high, Most reaches into the abdomen and pulls out reams of pale white intestines. "This is the best part of the job." He grins. "Hands're warm!" On the ground, the blood freezes so quickly little of it seeps into the snow. It is a dusky, purplish red; in the wind, our stiff faces assume the same hue.

When the pig is cleanly eviscerated, Mack again dons his gloves and hoists the saw. It has frozen, and he works it back and forth until it breaks free. Beginning at the tail, he halves the pig, drawing the saw downward, stopping just short of the nose. Now Mack, George and the butcher wrestle the V'd pig into a large plastic bag that balloons and crackles in the wind. As they heave the pig toward the butcher's truck, the men are thrown off balance. The hooks have frozen in the hocks. The boom is lowered, and with much grunting, the hooks are twisted free. The pig disappears into the truck bed.

The second pig goes even more quickly. George helps by kneeing the hide away from the suspended body. I notice the kidneys remain in each pig. "I pop 'em and leave 'em in the carcass," says Mack. "Gotta leave 'em for the state inspector." The kidneys are used to gauge the general health of the animal; scarring or other abnormalities indicate an underlying problem, and the meat may be condemned. In some cases, the twin organs are so visibly damaged that Most condemns the animal on the spot. Farmers losing a hog this way have been known to curse him roundly; of course, they do not realize how well Most understands the price of bad kidneys.

Soon we are back on the road. Our second appointment, a single hog, is thirty miles away. I express surprise at the speed of the butchering process compared to time spent on the road. "Hogs, we've done five an hour," says Most. I ask him about the process of killing an animal. "I'd rather shoot a pig with 'em lookin' at me," he says. Again, there is no irony in his voice. "Sometimes if you shoot 'em behind the ear, the bullet goes all the way through and ricochets around the barn." Indeed, at our next appointment, the bullet left the pig's skull and dented the gate.

Whereas the first farm we visited was neat and spare, the second was cluttered and largely in disrepair. The wind hurled itself unchecked through gaping holes in the haymow. In the yard it whipped and twisted through a maze of pallet stacks, discarded truck parts and outdated speedboats. We found the pig easily, but the farmer refused to have it shot in the barn. "He doesn't want blood in there," said Mack. "It can get the other pigs to attack each other." Three feet outside the barn door, the pig blinks and snuffles in the light, and turns toward Most. *Whap*.

Most has killed thousands of animals. He has no specific number, just "thousands." Yet, skinning another steaming pig, he hardly personifies death, clad as he is in a faded orange snowsuit, one leg of which is held together by copious twists of silver duct tape. Contrary to the popular perception of the burly butcher, Most is a slight man. His hands are scarred and thickened enough to reflect his profession, but his gold wedding band fits loosely over a small ring finger. Even a dark ski mask fails to lend an air of the sinister. Except when he is in the teeth of the wind, the mask is pushed up from his face, piled atop his head in loose rolls, a lackadaisical turban.

On the way home, the turban is riding high, and Most is in a storytelling mood. "Wanna hear a myth?" He grins for the fortieth time that day. "I knew an old farmer could predict the winter by the spleen of a hog. You fold the spleen in half. That's halfway through winter. Then you measure the width and the thickness from there. This winter was supposed to be warm in the middle, then get cold with a lot of precipitation." It is exactly the kind of winter we have had.

"Have I ever shot the wrong animal? Yes. Farmer said, 'That's the one . . . I think.' By the time he said 'I think' it was too late." His grin grows wider, and he shoots a sidelong glance. "Don't say: 'I think'!

"Sometimes this is like a rodeo. I been chased. Two weeks ago, one of Scooter Shystacker's longhorns, she was tempermental—that's why they had her done—come after me. Run her horns along that gate like a kid with a stick. She came after me and I jumped up in the truck and shot her."

"Sheep now, in the slaughterhouse, we use electrocution," he continues. George perks up. " 'Member that time I shocked one, and four of 'em dropped?"

"I've done C-sections," says Mack. "In a cow, you've got two minutes. I like to get 'em out in about forty-five seconds. You've got to tie the umbilical cord off and cut it, and then slit the cow's throat. It's kind of a good thing to bring one in the world after all the ones I've taken out."

As we near town, talk turns to Most's daughter. "She's six years old and weighs thirty pounds," he says. "Her kidneys were all full of scar tissue." He gives a detailed report of the surgeries she has undergone, the medications she must take daily to maintain her fragile state. "She's died on us twice," he says. "One time at home. I gave her CPR. It's a day-to-day thing."

It's still only 11:00 a.m. when we turn off Main Street and back the trailer behind the shop. Most disappears inside as I gather my things. As I step to the door to thank him, it swings open with a rush, and he strides into the cold sunlight. "Got another one!" he says. "Over by New Richmond!"

It is a fair distance to New Richmond. I ask if there will be time to do this and still make the two-hour drive to the hospital in Minneapolis. He answers over his shoulder, on the move. "I think I can make it!"

Of course, he is grinning.

1999

☺ ☺ ☺

P.S. In 2004, Mack's daughter received another kidney (her first came from Bob the One-Eyed Beagle, last seen singing karaoke in the last chapter of *Population 485*). As of this writing she was doing well.

Mack still works as a traveling butcher, but has retired the slaughter trailer in favor of a truck formerly used by a commercial weighing company. The portable scale apparatus included a steel beam that protrudes from the rear of the truck. It's perfect for hoisting carcasses.

The Fat Man
Delivers Christmas

December 1994. Two weeks before
Christmas. The Fat Man and I roll into
Hendersonville, Tennessee. We're hauling precious cargo, and the townsfolk line up along
Highway 31 to wave us in. They get right up
close, but I believe I have the best view, right
there in the plate-sized rearview mirror of that
Silver Eagle: fifty-three tour buses, ponderous
and sleek (most belonging to country music
artists, but a few the property of drivers on the
NASCAR circuit), curving out of sight behind
us, snaking through the darkness like a giant
string of holiday lights towed down the slow
lane by the very hand of God. Garth's bus is
back there, and Wynonna's. Reba sent one,
and so did Brooks & Dunn. The marquees at

the brow of each vehicle read like the weekly Top 40. But this
parade isn't about big names. This parade is about kids, and
Christmas. And it's about people like the Fat Man.

The bus driver they call the Fat Man was born Gene Reed.
Been driving a bus for thirty-one years. He's hauled Ferlin
Husky, Nat Stuckey, George Jones, Mel Tillis, the Forrester
Sisters, Joe Stampley, Brother Phelps, Ricky Van Shelton,
Van Halen, Kiss, 2 Live Crew, MC Hammer, Boyz 2 Men.
Voice like a Dixie back road: all gravel and drawl. A racon-
teur's love of holding the stage. Quick on the trigger with an
infinite range of ripostes, nearly all of them unprintably
earthy. And one of the founders of Christmas Is for Kids, the
event that drew me to Hendersonville. Christmas Is for Kids
began in 1981 when Reed and a group of nine buses arranged
to transport twenty-five disadvantaged children to a special
Christmas dinner and shopping trip. The volunteer efforts of
the drivers, artists, and chaperones, combined with the coop-
eration of regional school officials, eventually transformed
the first humble outing into a major event. The buses rolling
through Hendersonville tonight carry 358 children. "We pick
up our kids and meet at the First Baptist Church," says the Fat
Man. "The church puts on a meal and entertainment. Santa
Claus is there. Then we come on up here with these buses in
a convoy. And man, they give us the street."

Outside my window, a parked pickup truck beeps and
flashes its lights. Our three young passengers are in the rear of

the bus—site of the artist's master bedroom—watching cartoons, so I wave from the copilot seat in their place. A small part of me hopes I'll be taken for a star.

Before we set off in convoy, the children were given an after-dinner tour of Trinity City. Formerly known as Twitty City, in honor of Conway Twitty, whose home was on the grounds, the expansive complex was soaked in white Christmas lights; every tree was incandescent, every structure was outlined in twinkles. I kept hearing the words "Look! Look!" The children wound their way around flickering garden paths, across miniature walk bridges spanning a manicured stream, through sheltered courtyards. Fairy-tale scenes were arranged in diorama at each bend in the path. Many of the children chattered noisily. Some darted out of line. A pair of children in snow jackets left the tour to fool around in a garbage can. A tiny child, hand engulfed by a driver's beefy palm, stood transfixed in the face of it all, head tipped back, mouth parted, eyes wide. I looked at that child, and my throat hurt.

We left through tall gates and walked to the buses.

A lengthy wait ensued while the convoy was organized and the police escort arranged itself. Our kids wrestled in the aisle, and Reed spotted them in the mirror. "Awright, you kids, cut it out 'fore I snatch y' nekkid 'n' blister yer butt!" The giggling never let up as they ran off to the television in the back of the bus, to watch *The Simpsons*. Impatient, Reed keyed his CB mike and sang, "Sha na na na, Sha na na na, move 'em on out." A sardonic drawl came back at him: "What'd you do with the money I sent you for singin' lessons?" Reed cut him off. "I took your wife out, and I shoulda took the singin' lessons!" He turned to me. "I guess he'll ask me *that* again." Throughout the evening, the CB babble of boisterous good ol' boy bluster never stopped. We finally got the OK to head out. Reed celebrated the move with a heartfelt ditty: "Rollin', rollin', rollin', although my ass is swollen . . ." The kids were still in the back.

Out on the road, the CB traffic continued.

"I'm on the right side of ya, hauler!"

"Don't put no Prevost bus in there!"

"Let's slow 'em down, get 'em t' gether, tighten up!"

"Them Prevost, they'll run ya crazy!"

"Aw, yer a walkin' crime against nature!"

"Slow 'em down up there, slow 'em down!"

"OK, awright."

We wound around a long bend and Reed pointed out the door to the mirror. "That's a mess o' buses, buddy."

The convoy reaches the Kmart on the east end of town. The buses arrange themselves diagonally, in rows. The children are met by volunteer chaperones and taken to the store. The previous evening, in the same parking lot, the public was allowed to poke around the buses, examine the airbrushed murals, plush carpets, gleaming makeup mirrors. The accumulated funds finance a shopping spree for each child. The Fat Man shakes his head. "You'd think you'd hand a child fifty dollars, seventy-five dollars, the first place they'd head would be the toy department. But most of 'em won't buy no toys— they'll buy 'em somethin' to wear . . . a pair of shoes . . . it's just somethin' amazing to watch, man. It kinda restores your faith."

It's not all joyous. Some of the older kids know what's going on. Inside the store, their gazes slide to the tiles if they catch you looking. They hunch their shoulders a bit, move over an aisle. A photographer has accompanied me on the trip. He has taken pictures of the buses, the convoy. Inside the Kmart, he can't bring himself to uncap his lens. But back on the bus, the little girl who has been riding with us rushes aboard to show her purchases, and her eyes are clear and bright as she displays a necklace for her teacher, a trinket for her brother. She allows as how she can't wait to give them away, and then bounces back to watch cartoons again. Her bag remains on the table. In addition to a few toys, it contains socks, a shirt, a pair of mittens. The Fat Man was halfway through a decidedly ribald anecdote when the little girl returned. He draws a slow breath. "You really wanna see happiness in sadness, pain and sufferin' turned to smiles. . . ." He trails off, the sentence, like the anecdote, left unfinished.

The Fat Man drops me off back at the First Baptist parking lot. In the rear of the bus, the children are dancing around the bed. They holler a Merry Christmas at the photographer and me, then go back to dancing. The photographer and I will drive all night. We have to be in northern Wisconsin by morning. "Keep 'er outta the buckwheat," hollers the Fat Man. He waves, and the pneumatic door closes with a hiss. The air brakes release, and the diesel swells. The bus swings in a wide circle and glides away.

Somewhere in the middle of the night, I suppose about Indiana, I tell the photographer about the child with the wide eyes. How I was suddenly at the edge of tears over the simple wonder of the image. I tell him how I can't get around the troubling thought that this night of fantasy might only highlight troubles at home. I tell him how I can't understand why all this goodness leaves me unsettled. The Fat Man sees happiness in sadness . . . somehow I've gotten it backward.

They came to Hendersonville again this year. Fifty-one buses. Three hundred and two children. And the Fat Man was there. He'd driven 165,000 miles since his last Christmas Is for Kids. Enough mileage to circle the earth six times and most of a seventh; endless miles spent fighting inclement weather, artless motorists, clutch-shredding grades . . . the clock. But when he pulled that land yacht into line and rolled it sweet and easy up Highway 31, it was smooth sailing.

Man, they gave 'em the street.

1995

Big Things

The literature of the crude, instinctual colossus appealed to an urban audience by virtue of exoticism and, perhaps, fanciful nostalgia, the implicit contrast between the American Adam and the cosseted society that craved word of his untrammeled exploits. The giant was always a significant other, from another kind of place.

—Karal Ann Marling, *The Colossus of Roads*

Thank you for your inquiry requesting information about our "Fiberglass People Attractors." Enclosed please find our price list and brochure showing some of the hundreds of items that we make. As you can see, we can make anything Large or Small.

—Jerome A. Vettrus, *president of FAST Corp.,*
in a letter accompanying sales brochures

I do want the FAST Corp. to know that we are very proud of the New Giant Skier Statue. We have already received a tremendous amount of publicity from the skier and know it will be a huge promotional asset now and always. Again we thank you for your fine and detailed work.

—*satisfied customer, in letter to* Jerome A. Vettrus

Big Boy stood six feet tall. Weighed three hundred pounds. Stood there grinning at Toledo with that double burger hoisted high, those big blue eyes round as bowling balls, those red-checkered overalls fit to bust, that flip pompadour big enough to surf. When the men—boys, really, ten of them—showed up in the darkness, Big Boy's expression never changed. They ripped his feet from the concrete; he kept grinning. They tossed him in the back end of a pickup; he kept grinning. When the truck pulled up to an apartment on the west side of Toledo, he was still grinning.

Then things got ugly.

"What're we gonna do with him?" said one of the men. A number of suggestions were made. None caught anyone's perverse fancy. After all, pulling stunts with the Toledo Big Boy wasn't somebody's big new idea. "Nine times out of ten, if the Big Boy is missing, he's usually down at the University of Toledo," restaurant manager David Nelson would say upon discovering his missing mascot. "During fraternity season, they do that as a prank." The ten men huddled again. Then one spoke.

"Chop him up!"

And chop him up they did. A hacksaw was secured. Fiberglass particles filled the air. Big Boy's head tumbled from his neck. Then an arm came loose, severed at the shoulder. Next, a leg. When the bone-hollow sawing sounds ceased, only Big Boy's hamburger remained intact.

In a macabre twist, the first to learn of Big Boy's death by dismemberment (after the bandits) were members of his own family. At Big Boy restaurants throughout Toledo, his brothers looked down in the pale first light of morning to see bits of their luckless relative at their feet. A head, an arm, a leg, each tagged with the message "Big Boy is Dead." At one restaurant, Big Boy's severed right buttock was discovered with a newspaper ad taped in place: "Strip Steak $2.29 a pound." Not a good way to start the day, espying bits of a family member in the yard. Nonetheless, the relatives have maintained their sunny dispositions. Grinning like Big Boys, all of 'em.

As often happens in cases where criminals show off, criminals feel the need to talk, and two weeks after Big Boy bit it, his killers were corralled. Big Boy was worth about four thousand dollars and it is safe to say that will be divided ten ways. It seems unlikely that anyone will do any hard time, although one of the suspects, a Mr. Martinez, may wish to do so and apply it toward his degree; he is a criminal justice major at the University of Toledo.

The point of this parable, however, is not the fate of the perps. Nor do I wish to further flog the fanciful notion of oversized fiberglass figure as decedent. The significance of Big Boy as part of colossal Americana kitsch, however, is worth pondering. Why did the abduction and subsequent mutilation of a mass-produced corporate logo attract national press attention in publications ranging from *People* to *The New Republic*? Why do we care about big things that really aren't big things at all? Would we have cared if someone abducted a set of Golden Arches? Hacked up an Arby's sign? Not likely. But take an object we are all familiar with, blow it out of scale, and suddenly we are fascinated by it. Or at least most of us are, the odd criminal justice major excepted. But why? In *The Colossus of Roads*, Karal Ann Marling offers the following considerations:

> *Regardless of its particular purpose, the colossus is always a place in itself——a stopping place in time, where the everyday rules of reality are suspended and an idyllic dream commences. Grotesque scale demands a pause——for edification, for commerce, or for the fantastic fun of it.*

The pause. That's it. That's why they stick giant Big Boys on top of restaurants. That's why the Freshwater Fishing Hall of Fame in Hayward, Wisconsin, is housed in a 145-foot-long, walk-through fiberglass muskellunge. So you'll pause. And when the good citizens of Rothsay, Minnesota, got together in 1976 and built themselves a nine-thousand-pound replica of a male prairie chicken posed in the throes of a mating dance, they for dang sure figured on getting people to pause. To quote Marling again:

> *The publicity value of roadside curiosities, it would seem, increases in direct proportion to their curiousness.*

Homemade nine-thousand-pound prairie chickens in love—now that's curiousness. But what qualifies as collosi? Marling sniffs at the idea of Big Boy as colossus. "He's actually quite small . . . six feet tall, I believe." Yes. But he weighs three-hundred-pounds and perches atop restaurants. As boys go, that's colossal.

Some colossi are unmistakably colossal. Like the fifteen-foot-tall Paul Bunyan built on the shore of Lake Bemidji, in Minnesota. The winter of 1937 had been hard on the citizens of Bemidji; the mercury plunged to record depths and took business with it. Alternately fretting and telling tall tales around backroom stoves, the locals hit upon an idea. Why not enlist the services of a tall-tale hero of the times, Paul Bunyan, to lure commerce back to the frozen Bemidji environs? And so the hardy Bemidjians whacked together an ungainly, oversized Bunyan. It worked. Paul (joined one year later by a giant mobile Babe the Blue Ox mounted on a Model A chassis) got people to stop. To pause.

In 1978, the citizens of Blue Earth, Minnesota, paused—together with the governor, Miss Minnesota, and Miss America—to watch as a fifty-foot Jolly Green Giant rose high over their little town. The Jolly Green Giant took his place on a hut-sized concrete pedestal right at the location and time the eastern and western ends of I-90, the longest freeway in America, were joined. The cars flying by on the clean white concrete had little reason to stop in Blue

Earth. Local merchants hoped the Giant would make the difference.

One of the largest and most uniquely functional colossi in America is the aforementioned hall of fame muskie in Hayward. Half a city block long and five stories tall, the "Giant Walk-Thru Muskie" dominates the hall of fame grounds. Visitors can ascend from within the fish to stand in its gaping maw, far above the ground. A number of couples have wended their way through the bowels of this gargantuan fish to be wedded in the lower lip. Looking into each other's eyes, the bride and groom pledge themselves to a lifetime of loving and cherishing while neatly framed by a predatory hedge of knee-high teeth.

If the Jolly Green Giant ate hamburgers, he'd probably want the one sitting in the grass along Highway 21, just east of Sparta, Wisconsin. Trimmed with cheese and fat dollops of ketchup, the burger is roughly the size of a Volkswagen. A few feet away, an ice cream cone large enough to hold Rush Limbaugh (sans ego) collects rainwater. The cone is shadowed by an elephant and two porpoises to the north. Atlas rises against the sky, crouched as though he had the weight of the world on his shoulders, despite the fact that the world lies in fiberglass pieces at his sandaled feet. Behind Atlas and his shattered world, a great unpainted menagerie ranges around a two-acre grassy clearing: reclining bears, laughing dolphins, a seal big as a steer, a steer big as a corncrib. A six-foot Michelob bottle is canopied by chokecherries. A twenty-five-foot tall "beach boy" lies flat on his back, with one hand extended to the sky. The hand is cupped in the form of a C, ready to cradle a giant can of beer.

Throughout the clearing, stacked and leaned amongst the figures, are strange husklike sections of fiberglass. From the outside, they suggest the shape of familiar things, but the lines are obscure and rough. Closer inspection reveals that the underside of each husk is finely detailed; these are the forms used to create six-foot six-packs, elephantine elephants, giant fish, giant giants—whatever your heart desires, in gargantua. Dropped at the feet of the creatures they created, the brownish forms take on the appearance of freshly shed exoskeletons.

Stepping through the exoskeletons, reconciling the adjacent Wisconsin cornfields with the presence of a supine, grinning whale, the curious visitor might likely overlook the narrow, unassuming concrete block shed at the edge of the field. Two large red fiberglass letters stand out against the white-painted blocks: F and A. Missing are an S and T; together the four letters stand for Fiberglass Animals, Statues & Trademarks. There have been three fiberglass companies in Sparta since the late '50s. The first, Stouffer's Advertising, originated as a sign company. When a California company hit upon the idea of promoting their restaurants with a sculpted caricature of an "all-American boy," Stouffer's got the job. Thus was Big Boy born, and thus did Sparta begin its run as the nation's primary source of fiberglass sculpture.

When Lady Bird Johnson crusaded to rid the nation's highways of all things unsightly during the late '60s, times got tough for billboard companies. Armed with their experience creating Big Boys, Stouffer's converted to the production of "dimensional animals and statues" exclusively. In 1975, the company changed hands and operated until 1983 as Creative Display. It was during this time that the Jolly Green Giant and giant muskie were created. In 1983, Creative Display artist Jerry Vettrus became president and owner of the firm, which then became known as FAST Corp.

"I got into it by accident," says Vettrus. His office is a narrow, cramped affair, stacked high with paperwork, scattered with statuettes of past and present projects. The walls are papered with pictures of his creations. And he did get into his profession by accident. It all began when he drew a picture of a dead dog.

"I had no formal training," he says. He is low-key and unassuming, but speaks with one eye on the clock, in the manner of a man who has much to do. "A friend's dog died, and he asked that I draw him a picture of it. I did. And then I was an artist. Eventually, I had some of my work for sale in a cafe, and the owners of Creative Display saw it. They asked me to do some artwork for them. Then in 1976 they asked me to run the plant."

Today, Vettrus has fourteen employees, and business is brisk—a fact over which he is mildly despairing. "I am a combination businessman/artist by necessity," he says ruefully, riffling a stack of government forms on his desk. "Of course I'd rather just be an artist."

The bulk of FAST Corp. business comes from water parks, which order trailerfuls of hippo drinking fountains, gorilla swings, crawl-thru fish, whale fountains, and turtle slides. The company also supplies figures for miniature golf courses, civic projects, playgrounds, lawn decoration, and national brand promotions.

Despite the fact that FAST has a collection of over five hundred molds, Vettrus receives roughly one dozen requests for new items each year. "You just tell me what size you want of it." He grins. When a new project is commissioned, the object is photographed from the front and side, then "blown up" using a system of grids. Next, the front and side profile cutouts are constructed in full size from five-by-twelve sheets of cardboard taped together. The cutouts are then joined at bisecting right angles and sprayed with carvable foam. The foam is sculpted (faces and hands are sometimes sculpted from clay for greater detail), plastered, spray painted, and then coated with wax. A fiberglass casting is then made. When it hardens, it is cut away. The original model is destroyed in the process.

A similar process is then used to make the actual statue. The cast form is sprayed with wax, then fiberglass. After removal from the form, the statue is trimmed and sanded, then painted. "We use automotive paint," says Vettrus, "so once they're done, we just bolt 'em down to the trailer and roll down the highway."

"I do more of the detail sculpting—hands and faces—and the painting," says Vettrus. "If you want to know more about the initial sculpting, you should visit Oz." "Oz," as it turns out, is longtime friend and fellow sculptor Dave Osborne. "He's out in the industrial park across town carving a twenty-five-foot gorilla."

Dave Osborne is in his fifties. He has been sculpting colossi of one form or another since 1962. "It's all I ever done," he'll tell you. Today he is standing on a stepladder, wielding an electric coping saw. Bits of foam cling to his sweatshirt, dot his hair, gather on his thick eyebrows as he carves out the waist of his twenty-five-foot gorilla. Across the workshop the gorilla's unfinished torso holds its arms high and wide, as if hoisting a gi-ant beer keg over its head. The sculpture is too tall for the building and must be constructed in two halves.

"My background, as far as the sculpting?" says Osborne, lowering his saw. "Ummm . . . nothing really. I learned to work with large size and shape through the billboard business. Learned how to scale things up. Nothing formal. I didn't take no schooling of any source." He is a stocky man, self-effacing but eager to describe his work.

"The hardest part is you got to have a photographic mind." He picks up an air wrench, presenting it in side and front view. "For instance, if you pick up an object like this and say, 'OK, make this ten feet tall,' that's fine, they can give you a picture of it and you can make the cutouts, but you still have to have a heck of an imagination what the missing parts look like. It's like this ape. Unless you have an ape sitting right here, you have to fill in the detail."

Then, as if he has made it all sound too difficult, he grins. "Aww, we just grid it up." He waves a dismissive hand. "It's just like building airplanes."

America, the country where we do everything bigger and better, seems a natural for colossi—and indeed, America does seem to have cornered the market on kitschy colossi, although Karal Ann Marling points out that second place in the colossus race traditionally goes to totalitarian regimes. "They don't tend to be popular. They are often designed to stun rather than impress. Saddam Hussein designed a Gulf War Memorial in the shape of giant hands holding a scimitar above the citizens of Iraq." I'll take the prancing prairie chicken, thanks.

But is there room for giant things in America anymore? Sometimes it seems most of our modern colossi are conceptual; the Internet is a perfect example. Will people still pull off the road to look at an acromegalic cow? Karal Ann Marling doesn't think so. "There are not a lot of new ones being built. We've gotten just a little more sophisticated than 'big equals interesting.'" But Vettrus and Osborne disagree. "We don't promote a lot, but every year it seems like we do something for a city or a community," says Vettrus. "Seymour, Wisconsin, is the hamburger capital of the world, and they just called me and want to rent our giant eleven-foot hamburger for three months this summer . . . and if they like it, they may end up buying it for the city.

"When they're traveling, people just love to stand next to something and have their picture taken. It highlights their trip and gives them a remembrance of where they've been. Something that's larger than life-size is interesting.

"It's a photographic thing."

Dave Osborne is standing beside an unfinished gorilla toe the size of a third-grader. You can't convince him the hunger for colossi in America has died. "It's simple. It turns heads. It's like the Big Boy they had there for a while. He had that hamburger . . . it was simple."

Despite the upbeat spin of Vettrus and Osborne, hints of change are afoot. Increasingly restrictive ordinances regarding signage have caused many Big Boy restaurants to opt for simple, one-dimensional illuminated emblems. The demand for full-sized Big Boys has tailed off, and FAST Corp. stopped making them several years ago. Back in Toledo, they've patched Big Boy the murder victim back together as best they can. His stomach and one ear are still missing, however, and out in front of the restaurant he so proudly represented, his concrete footprints remain unfilled.

1996

○ ○ ○

P.S. Nine years later, I hereby retract the Rush Limbaugh line. Not that Rush requires defense, the line just isn't that good. It's disingenuous, easy, and instantly dated. Giggles for comments of this sort emanate chiefly from the choir loft and are thus discounted. Furthermore, once you call someone a big fat idiot, you have lowered the level of your discourse to the point that you will only regain the high ground by crawling.

The Roots Remain

War is a morally repulsive business, and
when the fog of battle clears, we are quick to
consign the details to history and myth. But
veterans are details who walk among us. I was
reminded of this one green morning a few years
ago, when I walked to my kitchen window only
to be startled by a tottering rank of soldiers ad-
vancing on my peonies. There were eight of
them, old men with rifles, one man bearing the
Stars and Stripes on a flagpole cantilevered off
his belt buckle. I gaped a moment, then recognized the troops as the local veterans color
guard, rehearsing for an afternoon funeral. The
back door of the Legion Hall and the back door
of my house open toward each other, and the
men of the post had turned the potholed alley
between us into a parade ground.

The Roots Remain

I find it difficult to address the subject of veterans without descending into star-spangled cliches. And so I treasure the off-kilter image of that benevolent morning invasion. I watched as they counted off their steps and fell in line, watched as the sergeant-at-arms commanded them to raise their rifles, to ready, aim, fire, watched them finish by snapping the steel butt plates to the ground. They worked the drill again and again. Frequently one or the other of them missed a command, jerking his rifle into place a beat behind, or sneaking a peek at the next guy in line in the manner of a child gone lost amidst the choreography of a grade-school Christmas pageant, trying to clue in and catch up without breaking the stiff posture formality requires. One of the men had difficulty standing at attention—now and then his rawboned frame was swept by a list and sway, as if he were a cattail bumped by a breeze. But they were game, and they kept at it until they got it right, and then they stowed their rifles and departed for the cemetery. Not long after, a wire story in the local paper reported that United States veterans were aging and dying at a rate—500,000 per year, according to some accounts—that made it increasingly difficult to field color guards like this one for ceremonies, funerals, and parades.

Five years passed, to a Monday morning last spring. I was upstairs writing and heard voices sifting through a backyard screen. I went to the window at the head of the stairs. It was the ragtag platoon, drilling again. They stood on the fringe of my grassy lot, hoisting and aiming their clunky rifles. I wondered who had died, then realized it was Memorial Day, which cast the question in an entirely different light. I thought of the newspaper article and, noting that the company before me had waned a man or two, made my way downstairs and out to the alley. I recognized the tall man who served as our village postmaster for twenty-one years. "Where you headed?" I asked. "Seventh Day church," he said. I felt silly and dissolute, standing there in my sandals and baggy shorts, corn-fed and safe and only accidentally aware of the significance of the day.

I had a quick shower and left for the church. On my way, I noticed a crowd had gathered down on the corner of Elm and Central streets, where Mack and Jack Most were taking down a big old spruce tree in someone's yard. It was a tricky job. The tree was surrounded on three sides by power lines, the solid trunk within easy reach of a house, and the top liable to land in the Security Bank parking lot if it fell wrong. Mack and Jack are identical twins, and around here, if you want a tree taken down in close quarters, you call the Most boys. It's a dangerous art, felling trees in confined spaces, requiring a seasoned mix of caution and derring-do. They had a few helpers, and a goodly audience of bystanders. I counted upwards of forty people sitting along the curb opposite, along the far side of the house, and on the steps of the United Methodist Church.

Three blocks will take you to the edge of this town no matter which direction you drive, and I was shortly at the Seventh Day Baptist church. We sat on folding chairs in the gravel parking lot, and there weren't many more than thirty of us, but they had to unfold a few more chairs for latecomers, and when the post commander adjusted his hearing aid and grasped the slim wooden lectern, he declared how pleased he was at the increased turnout. But then he recalled when Memorial Day meant bands and marching, and a parade that wound down Central Street and turned up Main, where the people waited in honorific rows. I wish, he said, we could get people interested again. The post chaplain offered a prayer, a retired butcher led us, a cappella, in the national anthem, and we recited the Pledge of Allegiance, which always reminds me of kindergarten and the flag at the end of Mrs. Amodt's blackboard. Reverend Susan rose in her calico dress to draw from the New Testament, and I know I should have paid closer attention, but I was listening to the superficial bustle of the cars out on the state highway, and the sparrows, and wondering at the passage of time, how it outlives men and their wars, but can't seem to cure us of fighting. Then Reverend Susan spoke of sacrifices made not for the present but for the future. Many of the fallen, she said, fell saying, "I care about those coming after me," and I wondered where that put me. Reverend Susan finished, and the post commander rose, only to have a swoop of wind knock the flagpole over his head, at which he grinned and allowed as how he'd never gotten a Purple Heart, and in a hopeful and impish voice, asked, "Did it draw some blood?"

Representatives of the Ladies Auxiliary read the poem "In Flanders Fields" and another poem described as being "from the newspaper." We sang "America the Beautiful," and I thought of Mrs. Carlson, our beloved elementary music teacher, gone now for some twenty years. It seems my every patriotic thought is tied to grade school. The post adjutant read a poem called "I Am Old Glory," and I thrilled to the historic cadence, although it had a line that went "I am on the side of God," and I've got to tell you that made me a little nervous. And then, over in the cemetery, the firing squad rose, and those four rifles cracked as one—no contingent of fresh-faced marines could have fired more crisply. There were, in the united reports, echoes of terror and pride, of men falling and mothers weeping, and the implication that some freedoms are earned, many are conferred, and not a few carry the scent of gunpowder.

I am hip to the dangers of nationalism, jingoistic flag-waving, and the glorification of war. It is difficult to reconcile our ironic postmodern culture, larded with cynicism and a sense of entitlement, with these aging warriors. It is even more difficult—assuming, as I do, that frequently neither God nor any moral force is on the side of Old Glory—to find hope in the remembrance of war, in the attrition and ignorance fostered by the passage of time, in the idea that more people clustered up to see a tree cut down than to honor the ghosts of freedom. But I reckon I'm thankful to live in a place where two guys with a chainsaw can outdraw the satellite dish for an hour, and I'm thankful a rickety group of back-alley irregulars marched through my yard to remind me that history grows toward the past, but it is born in the present—a fact that implicates each of us in the shape of the future. The old soldiers fade away, taking their wars with them, leaving us to do what we will with the spoils.

Back on the corner of Elm and Central, all that remains of the spruce is a flat stump, cut flush to the ground. The family who owns the house just had twins—they need room to add on. Majestic as it was, the tree had to go, and so the Most boys took it down. The roots, of course, remain, spreading wider than the boughs ever did, holding their ground, a testament to things given, and taken.

2000

Taking Courage

A magazine requested essays composed in the wake of September 11, 2001. The name of the magazine is *Hope*.

◌ ◌ ◌

This is a message in a bottle. I send it from a peaceful little island, a cabin in the woods, built by my brothers when they were young. I am the oldest, but their competence—with tools, with machinery, with their hands—surpassed my own long ago. It is October, but the mercury will drop well below freezing tonight. Every half hour, I stoke the stove. The cabin is simple, solid, and square. Chinked with concrete. The hand-peeled logs still as Buddha. There are three sounds: the ruffle and snap of the fire, the hiss of the lantern, and the clack of my Smith Corona Classic 12.

This cabin sits on ground I memorized from childhood. I lock myself in here when the words aren't coming. Or when I need to face down the black dog. The bare logs, the wooden chair and table, the silence—they force the necessary confrontations. There are Thoreauvian overtones, but I'm really not much of an ascetic. Some of my best writing and thinking I do all hopped up on Little Debbie Zebra Cakes and black coffee, listening to three-chord roots rock. Tonight, though, I have a craving to unplug and go acoustic.

I wonder what we know now. Now, the moment you are reading this. The tumblers have been set in motion. Every second is a forking path. As I write, the woods are dark, save for the pale daubs of lantern light angling out the cabin windows. It seems like Earth might be rotating around this coordinate. It is stunning to think of all humankind made contiguous by the globe. It is difficult to think in terms of governments, of man's inhumanity to man. It is earthen and peaceful here.

Where I live, we were looking east all day That Day. Through the television, over the Web, with an ear to the radio. We peered through the smoke and the flags and began to get a sense of magnitude. In a faraway city, skyscrapers were falling—would the tremors reach our little township, where the only structure over two stories is a four-legged water tower?

Our volunteer fire department met for training the following evening. There are twenty-four of us, amateurs playing at a game in which the professionals regularly get their tails whipped. Flipping through *Firehouse* magazine before the meeting, I saw that 102 firefighters died in the line of duty in the year 2000. One rumbling instant in New York, and that number was eclipsed. The last burning structure I crawled into was a trailer. We were looking for a guy who turned out to be gone. Until courage meets circumstance, there are no heroes.

Tell me: How is the nation's resolve? Very few volunteer firefighters quit the department at the sight of big flames. They quit when they realize the bulk of the battle is a back-breaking slog. Hours spent burrowing and hacking through soggy debris to extinguish intransigent little hot spots. You begin a warrior and wind up a drudge, rolling hose, cleaning equipment, restocking the rigs. The September 11 attacks were nationally iconic. Our response was equally so. Unity. Strength. Charity. But the battle will not always live up to the telethon. Resolutions of substance generally require heavy lifting and extended attention to the mundane. I reckon I'm a pickup-truck-coveting blue-collar capitalist, but this talk of preserving the nation through the wielding of credit cards and the acquisition of king cabs at 0 percent APR makes me snort. It's hard to know what more—if anything—will be required of us. I'm not overly worried. My neighbors have already crawled through fire with me.

An East Coast friend said she figured I'd be hearing a lot of rural tavern talk of how it was time to kick some towel-head ass. Well, sure. There's always some loudmouth eager to swab the flag around like a World Wrestling Federation banner. But I have heard equivalent sentiments expressed on NPR and CNN, refined only in terms of diction and dress. Bigotry and extremism have commonality: Both are difficult to eradicate; both respond poorly to benevolence; and both are an embarrassment to those impugned through putative association, whether we wear NASCAR caps or turbans. The battle for civility will outlast all others.

My people are farmers and loggers and hunters. I grew up slinging manure—the metaphorical basis for a writing career. Thousands have died, bombs are falling, and in response, here I sit composing an essay: I feel as if I am throwing cotton candy at a steamroller.

I cherish my spot on our little fire department because if something is burning, we put water on it. Action over postulation. A week after the first attacks, we were alerted by Naval Intelligence that terrorists were thought to be targeting fire trucks for theft and use as car bombs. The intelligence was later revised, but we took some measures. One of us can sit down there with a deer rifle, if need be. I will say it's a heck of a thing to have Naval Intelligence briefings arriving in rural Chippewa County, Wisconsin. A shame and a comfort, really: The tremors spread.

By morning, the woodstove is dead cold. It takes a little internal dialogue to get me to unzip my army surplus sleeping bag. I stow the Smith Corona under the bunk and shoulder my backpack. When I come out of the woods, I hear Osama bin Laden say there is fear in America. So be it. Courage does not arise out of comfort.

2001

Houses on Hills

The good building makes the landscape more
beautiful than it was before that building
was built.

—*Frank Lloyd Wright*

It was the ship-shaped house that
finally did it. In the space of a few short
months, it came plowing over the crest of a
formerly mapled hill, the beveled two-story
prow of the living room looming into the skyline like a grounded destroyer jammed atop a
sand dune. During my weekly comings and
goings, I watched it take shape, and wondered
what had moved the owner to choose this
particular site. Ego, perhaps, an ostentatious
hankering to let folks know that this particular
American dream was charging right along. But
if conspicuous consumption explains the view

he's given us, it hardly explains the one the owner has chosen for himself: a glittering, bi-level bank of garage-door-sized windows affording an unobstructed, panoramic view of . . . the freeway. On any given summer weekend, the owner of this nautical monstrosity can chill a drink, retire to the balcony, and review an endless parade of Illinois tourists pell-melling their way north.

In his recent book, *Mapping the Farm* (Knopf), author John Hildebrand refers to this new trend in home building as the "look at me" school of architecture. By my definition, look-at-me hill houses are largish new homes constructed on former farmland, atop hills. The trend seems to be to hack a square out of the tree line, deposit the house, and dam the horizon. In even more egregious instances, there are no trees at all; the house squats solo on the skyline, subtle as a gopher mound on a putting green.

People are entitled to displays of bad taste. Heck, I'm the last person to judge someone on matters aesthetic—me, sitting here in my sweatpants in a one-armed office chair at a discount-chain desk constructed of particleboard and wood-grain contact paper. But at least I'm not perched on a hill beside the interstate, big as a house. It's one thing to exhibit a complete lack of style and grace in the privacy of your own home. It's entirely another thing to do it at the expense of everyone's landscape. These people don't want to be part of the horizon, they want to *be* the horizon. Why nestle in the valley when you can frame your success with the sky?

Let me take another tack. There is a river near here that is corralled for several miles on one side by steep pine bluffs. Recently, the bluffs have become studded with so many look-at-me hill houses I am reminded of Germany's Rhine Valley and its range of cliff-topping castles. Which might give the owners of today's ersatz chateaux pause for thought, as the castles along the Rhine were stormed at fairly regular intervals. Most of the ones I've visited had been torched or shot up pretty good. Often more than once. At a time when the gulf between the haves and have-nots gapes wider yearly, the day may not be so far off when making what you "have" as obvious as a castle will be unwise. Something to ponder while sitting in your A-frame at eye level with the eagles.

Of course, all of this is little more than amateur armchair grumbling on my part. The topic cries out for a more informed opinion—the opinion, say, of a renowned landscape architect.

Now, I'm no renowned landscape architect, but I read an article about one once. In *The New Yorker*, no less. His name was Dan Kiley. According to the article, he was eighty-three years old last year, and has been described as "the reigning classicist in landscape design." It has also been said that he "has done more than anyone else in his field to lead American landscape architecture back to its classical roots: to formal geometry; to the axis, the allee, the bosquet, the terrace, the *tapis vert* . . ."

I wouldn't know *tapis vert* from Diet Squirt, but I do know ugly when I see it, and so, when I saw the boathouse, I fired a letter off to Mr. Kiley. Can you spare me a note, I asked, detailing your thoughts about this disturbing trend? I would love, I wrote, to compare my reaction (no doubt a sort of visceral parochial protectionism on my part) to your more artistically and professionally informed opinion.

And I'll be darned if he didn't write back. A one-paragraph note, but it did my farm-boy heart good:

Office of Dan Kiley
Landscape Architects and Planners
20 November 1995

Dear Michael Perry:
It does not take an esoteric professional to explain the observation that you make. Simply stated, people are disconnected from the land; there is no tradition to guide them to do the right thing by the land. Inappropriate and insensitive developments are not restricted to country areas, they are also found in the suburbs and cities.

Sincerely,
Dan Kiley

And so, my amateur grumblings validated, I feel bold enough to issue the following appeal (I don't mean to speak for Mr. Kiley, but I reckon we are in agreement on this): If the American free enterprise system has been good to you, by all means build yourself a dream house with all the doodads. I'm all for that. But do Dan and me a favor:

Stick it *behind* a hill.

1996

◌ ◌ ◌

P.S. Rereading this piece nearly ten years later, I remain unmoved on the subject in general, but feel the tone I took with the owners of the "ship-shaped" house was frankly snotty. What did I know of their hopes and struggles?

I did find that an essay like this pretty much guarantees you will meet people who own houses on hills. My ophthalmologist, for instance. He usually waits until my eyes are dilated and I am unable to drive or negotiate hallways before he starts in on me.

Dan Kiley died February 21, 2004.

Swelter

Bits of this essay appeared in the opening chapter of *Population: 485*.

○ ○ ○

I was young when the streaking fad hit. Mid–grade school, maybe. Sinful, I thought. But I had a go at it. Dropping our clothes beside the sinkhole in the sheep pasture, a friend and I took off across the field, chasing his horse, Daisy. Daisy had been trained for the circus. You could vault to her back from behind. We never tried that with our clothes off. It seems ludicrous now, the image of two hairless children capering through the fat alfalfa, forty acres from the nearest road, with no one to see us but my younger brother. Even then more sensible than I, he sat at the edge of the sinkhole, nibbling a bird-legged stem of canary grass. He knew we weren't raised that way. And we weren't. So after a lap or two, my friend and I put on our jeans, adjusted our T-shirts to our tan lines, and ascended the lower limbs of popple trees, jackknives open, to mark the day in the bitter bark. I haven't disrobed in public since.

But I know why we stripped that day.

Blame summer.

Summer is a seducer. After bundling through another tight-lipped winter, after enduring the mounting frustration of spring's titillating dance of veils, we gape as summer comes sliding down her blazing ecliptic like a woman down a bannister. She laughs with her head thrown far back; she throws her hands high in the air, releasing fistfuls of butterflies. She belly dances through the cornfields until the dust rises like a charmed snake, hanging in fat curls, leaving you cotton-mouthed. She makes the fox pant, she drives the hawk to thin air. Weaker creatures curtain themselves away to complain.

"Can't stand this," say people who only months ago chattered and whined in the cold. "It's not so much the heat . . . ," they mewl, their humidifiers sagging and worn to a frazzle, tattered after cranking out a ceaseless fog against winter's moistureless air. Give me summer. Give me dappled cattails sashaying under a breeze so like hot breath it stirs unclean thoughts; give me warm ditches all clotted with frog eggs, sunning turtles, wheezing nights. In the summer we live dangerously, driving fast with our vulnerable elbows out the window. We loosen our clothes, make love with the screens open. Summer makes us fearless. One summer I was twelve hundred miles from home. I wrote a brave letter to a girl I didn't know. When I returned, a few hot days of August remained. Beneath a moth-clogged porch light, she took my face in her hands and kissed me.

In the summer, sweat is easily earned, rising at the slightest provocation. In the haymow, alfalfa chaff with the scent of toasted tea plasters at the hollow of a farmer's neck; his forearms ripple shiny and green. Over dishes in the kitchen, his wife turns her wrist, runs it across her brow.

Summer taunts the weak. Morning glories rise early like pious old women to prayer, pale purple and cool to the touch. But by midmorning faith fails them; they purse their lips and retire frowning to their clinging vines. In the meantime, summer has taken over the day, driving sheep to shade. Sparrows wallow in the dust, and horses stand wide-legged and motionless, heads down. She has built a heavy heat, summer, a heat with momentum. Momentum to carry well into the night, where it will pad the air, squat above the sheets, dim the stars.

Like any decadent creature, summer shows her age prematurely. As early as July the greens assume a harder edge. Blight stains the popple leaves, the timothy grows stalky and thin. Like a thickening woman, one halter top strap off the shoulder, like a man adjusting his thin hair while his sports car idles, there is evidence that summer is going to seed, leaving you to nurse regret through the fall, the season of penitence. Fall is penitence. Winter is abstinence. But the cycle is a circle, and fasting sharpens hunger. By springtime, you are ready to sin again. And summer will oblige you, whistling like a torch, flaming and shameless, with the power to make young boys strip naked and dance for the sun.

We grew apart, my streaking friend and I. He graduated, and a year later I left town. There were rumors of trouble, then rumors of his being born again. One humid day a year ago, I drove by his house and there was nothing out front but a rusty truck. His windows were tightly shut. I thought it symbolic: summer, heavily made up and waiting in the yard; him having none of it. I was overreaching, of course, imposing metaphor to serve my own purpose. It turns out he runs a business reclaiming concrete silos—exhausting, dangerous work performed high above barnyards. While I hunker beneath a roof, rearranging words in an attempt to capture summer, bring it inside, he is out in it, the sun hot on his bare back, baking him like the unpicked stones in the fields below.

We ran into each other at the local gas station recently. He tossed a carton of cigarettes through his truck window and came over to talk. We caught up a bit, him with his sunburned, work-skinned arms folded across the front of a sleeveless T-shirt, me in my clean jeans. I didn't bring up the streaking, didn't ask him to comment on my attempts to characterize summer as sensuous seducer. He did mention that he sometimes travels to South America in the winter. He didn't say why. I'd like to think summer draws him down there. The temptress, that sort of thing. But I suspect he has other reasons, and another metaphor withers.

And so in the end, summer is simply warm weather. For all this pungent talk of sweat and seduction, I believe summer is understood only by the child too young to be troubled by the adult inferences of nakedness and heat, unfettered by metaphor and allusion, content simply to sprint through the grass and get about this business of growing old under the sun.

1998

You Are Here

Any pilot who has gone off course while "flying on visuals" knows what it is to dip from the clouds to reconnoiter the earth. To search for an orienting feature in the landscape below, a landmark that says, "You Are Here." Imagine then, how welcome the sight of a water tower, standing out like a giant pushpin stuck in a topographical map, clearly labeled with the name of the community arranged about its base.

We most commonly see water towers from ground level, often while traveling, but they are no less a source of orientation to us than they are to the pilot. From the perspective of the road, a water tower becomes a giant signpost representing a community. "Here we are," say the residents of Richmond, Indiana, all day and all night, thanks to their illuminated roadside tower. "Here we are," say the residents of Beebe, Arkansas, adding in painted epigraph, "Your Dream Hometown." Here we are, in spite of everything, declared Florida City, Florida, in 1992, after Hurricane Andrew peeled the *F* and *C* from the silver skin of their water tower, but failed to topple it. Here we are, if you look closely, says the water storage tank in Bedminster, New Jersey, its walls camouflaged with trees in silhouette.

Even when the road you travel is cybernetic, many of the towns you approach choose to introduce themselves via their water towers. Journey to the Hartington, Nebraska, Web page and you'll see a simple, captionless photo of its colorful tower, looking overdressed and lonely on a plain. Denison, Iowa, presents a thumbnail photo of its million-gallon tower, and explains that the painted caption, "It's a Wonderful Life," is in honor of Denison native Donna Reed for her most famous film appearance. Go north of the border to Red Deer, Alberta, Canada, select the water tower page, and while no picture pops up, you will be able to learn from the text that the tower is "big" and "green." Moreover, "you may be interested to know that the water tower has never leaked." Knoxville, Illinois, shares a photo and the information that the water in its tower is "naturally fluoridated and slightly radioactive."

"Here we are," say water towers on behalf of a community, "and this says something about us."

My hometown water tower stands just off Main Street,

along the soft descent leading from the freeway overpass to the old, underfed highway at the center of town. Built in a style the experts refer to as "double ellipsoidal multicolumn," it exhibits a solid stance, the four slim legs angling outward a bit as they drop from their attachment at the convex belly of the silver-gray tank. Simple block letters, spare and black, follow the curvature of the sidewalls, peeking from behind the wraparound catwalk: NEW AUBURN. The cap, a meniscus of steel, is crowned with a small American flag. During the holiday season, a star of lights joins the flag. A black-and-white picture of the tower, taken shortly after its construction in 1950, hangs in the village hall. It might have been taken yesterday. When I roll up the exit ramp from the freeway, I enjoy the thought of people approaching town back when the old highway was in its heyday, seeing the same water tower, albeit from the opposite direction. More than the houses, more than the streets, more than the small green sign at the outskirts, it has always been the sight of the water tower that has told us, "here you are."

No less an authority on American culture than Garrison Keillor has reinforced the image of water tower as icon. Winners of *A Prairie Home Companion*'s "Talent from Towns Under 2000" contest tote home a trophy modeled after the witch-hatted steel towers that dot Minnesota's plains. Keillor himself chose the image and sees it as symbolic of small-town America.

Keillor's frame of reference is Midwestern, and that frame of reference is telling. For someone raised in the heartland, it's easy to think of the old silver water tower as definitively iconic. Of course, this is not so. In Ypsilanti, Michigan, water has been stored since 1891 in a 147-foot-tall stone and concrete tower. A tower standing in Coral Gables, Florida, is disguised as a lighthouse of Spanish-Moorish architectural extraction, with a sundial attached to its south face. In Mendocino, California, a tower constructed in 1857 to serve the Carlson City Hotel still stands. Constructed of redwood, it has the appearance of a tall rectangular box, capped with a flat pyramid of shake shingles. In 1870, the hotel was destroyed by fire, but the tower endured. One year later, the Chicago Water Tower survived the Great Chicago Fire. Constructed of limestone in a style referred to as "naïvely Gothic," the tower includes turrets, battlements and slit windows with architraves. Topping it all off is a green copper cap. In 1969, the American Water Works Association chose the Chicago Water Tower as its inaugural American Water Landmark. Consequently, one of the first water towers officially designated as classic had no legs; it was crenellated, not witch-hatted.

In 1895, Jacob Miller built a limestone water tower in Clinton, Wisconsin. The tank was made of wood; when fluctuations in the weather caused leaks, residents turned out to hand-tighten the turnbuckles. Wooden tanks were still being constructed in the 1950s; you're most likely to spot one in

New York, Philadelphia, and on the Chicago skyline. Early steel towers were patched together with riveted panels. But by 1930, welding had replaced riveting.

The smooth surface of welded tanks is easier to maintain, and welding allows a versatility of design not possible with riveted construction. The intricate detailing of the 100,000-gallon pineapple that stood atop the Dole Cannery in Honolulu until it was dismantled in 1993 is all the more remarkable for the fact that Chicago Bridge and Iron constructed it in 1927, using the riveting method.

Today, water storage vessels are classified in three configurations: reservoirs, standpipes and elevated tanks. A reservoir is generally a tank with a diameter greater than its height. Relative simplicity of design keeps fabrication costs low; however, reservoirs must be constructed on high ground if water is to flow by gravity.

A standpipe is defined as a tank that rests on the ground but has a height greater than its diameter; in other words, if a reservoir is a tuna can, a standpipe is a pop can. The extra height is used to create pressure for water distribution. The oldest steel standpipe in continuous use is located in Dedham, Massachussetts. Built in 1881, the Dedham tank tops the Steel Plate Fabricators Association's "Century Club," a list of twenty-two steel water storage tanks that have been in continuous service for over one hundred years.

Elevated tanks—true water towers—are subclassified by

style and capacity. In addition to the double ellipsoidal version that stands in my town, two other common variations include spherical single pedestal tanks (the ones that resemble giant mushrooms) and fluted column tanks, featuring a broad, fluted central support column beneath a tank shaped like an aspirin tablet.

There are deviations from the standards. Gaffney, South Carolina, promotes the peach trade with the "Peachoid," a million-gallon peach-shaped tower replete with twelve-foot stem, sixty-foot leaf, sculptured cleft, and even a peachy little nipple. Built by the Chicago Bridge and Iron Company and painted by artist Peter Freudenberg, the Peachoid has its own Web site and has even been touched by scandal (owing to the remarkable resemblance of another town's copycat tower). A water tower in Plant City, Florida, is shaped like a giant strawberry. Another in Germantown, Maryland, is a spherical simulacrum of the earth viewed from space. Water towers have been constructed in the shape of apples, milk bottles, ketchup bottles, baby food jars, Dixie Cups, Mickey Mouse, a cake with candles. A giant coffee percolator in Stanton, Iowa, honors hometown girl Virginia Christine, the Mrs. Olson of Folgers coffee fame. More than one country club has erected a water tower painted to look like a golf ball perched on a tee.

But of course, no matter the shape, the color, or the message, a water tower's first purpose is to store water. Or, more specifically, to store energy: Pump stations along the line re-pressurize larger water systems, but in smaller systems, grav-ity alone forces water through the pipes. And so, in my town, the nearer your tap to the tower, the less time it takes to top off your teapot.

A tower also equalizes supply and demand. During peak water use—generally between 6:00 p.m. and 10:00 p.m.—demand may outstrip pumping capacities. The difference can be made up from storage. Then, when demand drops below average—generally from 10:00 p.m. to 7:00 a.m.—reserves are replenished. The ability to draw from reserves also allows your town to save money by running pumps during off-peak electricity demand periods, when power is cheaper. And storage reserves are essential in the event of a fire, when fire-fighting efforts can rapidly exceed normal peak demands.

Have you ever closed a tap abruptly and heard the water pipes clunk? That's "water hammer." Water hammer occurs when pumps switch on and off, or valves open or close. Sur-prisingly powerful pressure surges result and can seriously damage pipes and equipment. Water towers help offset water hammer damage, channeling the surges up the riser, where it is absorbed in the tank.

There is, in America, a cultural corps d'elite of sorts, a fraternity salted throughout the generations, the members of which, likely near the age of their emancipation, took a trip to the top of the town water tower. Most carried paint and left behind the classic "Class of . . ." inscription. Others, in the process of declaring undying love, foresight clouded by infatuation and euphoric chutzpah, left behind incriminating initials. A recent initiate (or team of initiates) in Archer City, Texas, eschewed tradition to address current, events. After city officials spent thirteen thousand dollars to repaint the water tower, they invested an additional one thousand dollars to install flat steel bars on the tower legs to thwart upwardly mobile graffiti artists. "Now," said a city representative, "if any kids climb up there, we're going to give them a spanking."

Shortly thereafter, the tank's defenses proved pregnable. The latest graffito? *You must give us a spanking.*

Arnie Napiwocki may have the answer to Archer City's problems. He is the owner of Lane Tank Company of Mosinee, Wisconsin. Much of his time is spent repainting water towers. It's an esoteric profession. "People who do elevated tank work are rare," he says. "Insurance is so expensive. . . . Workman's comp is way, way up there." In 1889, when construction workers were erecting a 147-foot tower in Ypsilanti, they invested in their own form of insurance by incorporating three crosses, still visible today, into the design.

Napiwocki's professional knowledge is laced with arcana: "Ambient air quality laws stipulate no one may put more than 5.7 pounds of dust into the air without a permit. The official definition of dust is any airborne material. That means if I drop a six-pound rock off your water tank, I'm in violation." It also means that prior to sandblasting paint containing hazardous compounds, he must wrap the entire tank in a tent—Christo has nothing on Napiwocki. He knows a tank must be emptied before he paints it. "Otherwise they sweat constantly."

He knows better than to emblazon a tank with "1996 State Football Champs" without a word of caution. "What about next year, when the girls volleyball team wins? And then the golf team? It can get expensive, and usually you're dealing with taxpayer money. Sometimes they're better off to just put up a sign."

And Napiwocki knows a thing or two about water tower graffiti. "It runs in cycles," he says. "Once it starts, it continues until the town cracks down." One of Napiwocki's regular customers, a small town in northern Wisconsin, recently suffered a rash of graffiti postings and hired Napiwocki to put obstructive gear at the base of the tower. "These kids rode by while we were putting the stuff up and said, 'We're going up there anyway.' I told them, 'Listen, this is costing your town a lot of money. Next time you go up there, just hang a banner.'

"A month later, the town called. They wanted me to come take a banner down."

• • •

Once a day, Rob, the village maintenance man in New Auburn, opens the door to a tiny brick hut at the base of the water tower. The interior is clean as a kitchen. Standing beside an electric pump motor the size of a pig, he takes the pulse of the system, checks dials and gauges and makes notes in a log. In the winter, he will be especially careful to check the condition of the circulating pump. If it fails unnoticed, a giant "ice doughnut" will form at the top of the tank. Come spring, it will shift and rip the steel as if it were tinfoil.

Twice a year, Rob climbs the tower to replace the flag. On his most recent ascent, the village board gave me permission to climb with him. What I saw surprised me. There was the old feed mill, there was the fire hall, there were our eleven streets. But this wasn't the town I thought I'd see. It appeared smaller—as if it could be gathered up in an armful—and yet at once more spacious. It seemed no distance at all from the tower to the implement store at the northern outskirts, and yet, cramped yards that can be crossed in twenty steps looked roomy and wide. There were sounds: the grating trundle of a child rolling down a driveway on a Big Wheel, a rumbling load of channel iron being trailered down Main Street, two women in backyard conversation, the yap of a dog, a table saw.

I circled the catwalk twice. Rob had already finished hanging the flag, and it was time to descend. Looking to the blue hills in the distance, I misstepped and leaned instinctively into the dense bulk of the tank. It felt cool, deeply solid. I thought

of all this water, fifty thousand gallons, forty-seven or so gallons of which—based on my water bills to date—I would
draw before the day was over. Water is life, and, as far as this
town is concerned, this is the source. This tank, with its un-
seen pulse, its cycles of filling and emptying, is our communal
heart, and threaded through the ground beneath us, to all
edges of the place we live, are the vessels, the arteries from
which we tap our own little daily portion.

Today, when I pass the tower and look to the catwalk, I
think of what I saw from that place above the ground but beneath the sky, and understand: *You are here.*

1997

♡ ♡ ♡

P.S. When compiling collections of this sort, one is chagrined to learn
how frequently one repeats oneself. For instance, it seems I have a
fascination for water hammer. I have mentioned it in at least three
different pieces of writing. Once here, once in *Population: 485,* and
elsewhere in these pages when referring to my personal plumbing.

As of this writing, there is talk of replacing the New Auburn water tower. I understand, but I will miss it.

II. Gearjammers

Convoy

If you accept the hypothesis posited via airbrush on the cab of a giant purple Freightliner idling behind a Nebraska truck stop, the American economy lives and dies on eighteen wheels: *Without Trucks, America Stops.* Evidence supporting the hypothesis? Virtually everything you purchased last year—whether you sat on it, wore it, listened to it, or ate it—was delivered by one of America's 3.1 million truckers. Trains, pipelines and ships move more bulk commodities, but in 1996, 60 percent of all domestic freight—6.5 billion tons—traveled by truck. Consequently, as the economy booms, so booms trucking. As of 1998, roughly 423,000 trucking companies were desperately competing for drivers at a rate projected to add between 40,000 and 80,000 new truckers to the road every year until 2005. A January 1997 *Time* magazine article ranked truck driving fifth on a list of the fifteen hottest fields.

But who wants to be a trucker? The associations are rarely flattering. The leering sleazeball in *Thelma & Louise*. The cold-eyed gear-jamming kidnapper in *Breakdown*. A goofy Sylvester Stallone, arm wrestling and dieseling a path to his son's heart in *Over the Top*. The Subaru Forester ad in the back of *Harper's*, with its beastly semi veering across the double yellow on a narrow mountain road (the family survives thanks only to the Forester's zippy, evasive all-wheel-drive system). The theme is repeated in any number of television commercials and rein-forced on the news: Trucks run the road like rhinos on a jail-break, usually with a spectacularly distorted passenger vehicle on their snout. And it doesn't help when some eighteen-wheeler looms over your trunk, filling your mirror with a palette of dried bug guts pasted across a steel bumper the size of a chromed morgue slab. Suddenly you are Dennis Weaver in Spielberg's *Duel*, strung on a thin wire between terror and defiance. You hold your own, because by God this is your road, too, but what a confidence builder it must be to sit eight feet above the concrete, backed by eighty thousand pounds of Big Mo. You look in the mirror again. I wonder, you think, what it's like up there.

And so you hitch a ride with a trucker.

The trouble with hitching a ride with a trucker is the lawyers. A truck wreck involving an unauthorized passenger is a litigation lollapalooza, and so most trucking companies have a no-riders policy. I knew this when I showed up with a backpack and a notebook at the Trucker's Jamboree in Waupun, Wisconsin, looking to hitch a ride on the Share America Convoy to Reno, Nevada. By the time I got to Dave Sweetman, I was batting oh-fer and expected to be turned down again. If you can't risk the liability, I said, I'll understand. He looked me over, then stuck a thumb over his shoulder. "See that?" I sighted along his thumb to the lettering on the side of his big green Kenworth. *Owned and Operated by David L. Sweetman, 3 Million Safe Miles.* He looked me square in the eye. "I reckon I can make it three million, two thousand." And so, we put our tin in the wind.

It's interesting what you feel up there in the prow of that big ship. Powerful, certainly, what with those 475 horses chooglin' along at your feet, the turbo holding its high, thin note, sucking down air, turning it into miles and blowing them out the twin stacks while the rest of the world sits still and falls behind. But you also feel a little tentative, a little out of control at the front end of all that length and momentum, like a flood victim sweeping downstream astride a duplex. And from up here, the cars—all of them, even the overblown

SUVs—look flighty and irresponsible. They take on the nature of pests, and when they dart too close, or linger too long in the vast blind spots, you want to chastise them, tell them to get clear for their own sake. They are like little piglets who fail to realize that while Mommy may wish them no ill, they must give her room to operate or risk being crushed.

As an owner-operator, Dave Sweetman owns his truck and leases his services to a car hauling company. Owner-operators are essentially self-employed. They enjoy more independence than company drivers, but they also have to keep a closer eye on the bottom line. Few are as established as Sweetman, and his truck, with all its accoutrements (including a stand-up shower), is not typical. Most truckers run with one eye on the road and one on the end of the month.

Sweetman's business card reads *Transporter Of New Rolls-Royce, Bentley, Ferrari, Lotus, Antique and Classic Cars, Trucks, Boats, Airplanes, Movie, TV and Celebrity Cars Door To Door*. He's hauled the Batmobile and the Fred Flinstone car. He's delivered cars to Puff Daddy, Lenny Kravitz, model Tyson Beckford, and spent quality time tooling around with Jay Leno. The priciest car he ever hauled was a 1907 Rolls-Royce Silver Ghost, otherwise known as "the World's Most Valuable Automobile." When Sweetman eased it into his trailer, it was insured for $40 million. It takes a confident man to handle that kind of cargo, and Sweetman is a bit of a showboat. At Waupun, his tricked-out truck won a rack of trophies for which he feigned apathy. He says things like "absol-tute-ly." He speed-dials his dispatcher on a voice-activated cell phone by barking "Butthead!" When he misspeaks, he lets loose a sharp tooth-whistle, as if he's summoning his runaway tongue, and cracks, "Brain-fade!" He's not cocky, but he operates with a contained swagger. Then again, he has navigated seventy-nine feet worth of Kenworth over enough miles to circle the earth 140 times—through twenty-five years of every imaginable form of ugly weather and ugly traffic, with nary a fender bender—all the while toting cargo valuable enough to finance a series of Whitewater investigations in perpetuity. There's a reason they've trusted him with the Silver Ghost six times in six years.

It's tough to recast the stereotypical trucker when he's all over the road. You don't remember all those trucks that run a polite line; you remember the one that squeezes you on a curve, the one that roars up and breathes down your neck, the one with the window sticker that reads "Diesel Fumes Make Me Horny." An hour at a truck stop will only reinforce the worst caricatures. Recurring themes: bellies, cigarettes, and scruffy disgruntlement, often clad in overdue laundry. These are impressions not easily overcome. You have to stand right up and acknowledge them, for starters, which means we must put Dave Sweetman on cruise for a minute and talk about Share America Convoy organizer Gary King. He knows what you think of truckers, and he knows why. "All our warts, wrinkles and bumps are out in the open," he says. "Whatever we do is pretty much observed." King is a former state trooper and Greyhound bus driver. Left all that to drive a truck for twenty-six years. Too many years behind the wheel, too many Camel cigarettes, and too much truck stop food have saddled him with short breath and swollen feet. He's a big man. "I'm two hundred sixty pounds, used to be three hundred. I can be as mean and nasty as anybody." But he smiles when he says that, because he has seen what mean and nasty have done to trucking. "The trucking industry was always known for having a brotherhood, and that's fallen by the wayside," he says. "There comes a time when you have to say enough is enough." What he really wants is for us all to get along, to buddy up and share the road. And so a few years ago, he started Trucker Buddy International, a pen-pal program linking drivers with grade school students. The truckers send letters and photos and souvenirs from the road, and drop by with their trucks now and then, and the kids learn about geography, and math, and commerce, and time, and distance. The kids would probably go bonkers if Shaquille O'Neal stopped by to play role model, but underperforming superstars are tough to book. Instead they get to meet a trucker who speaks with enthusiasm about a fundamental profession with no cheering section, and, as Dave Sweetman will tell me later, find out where potatoes come from. "Drivers have very few opportunities to give something back to society," says King, "even though they do it every day just by doing their job. This industry is the industry all others rely on." He hopes the convoy will help recruit drivers for the Trucker Buddy program, but he also hopes it will do a little something to re-hab the image of the American trucker.

Trucking was born at the end of the nineteenth century, when gasoline engines began to replace horses. In 1912, a Packard truck delivered three tons of freight from New York City to San Francisco—in forty-six days. Trucking was held back by a dearth of decent roadways until the Great Depression: President Franklin Delano Roosevelt responded to the economic crisis with work-relief programs, the largest of which was road building. The modern age of trucking arrived in 1956, courtesy of President Dwight Eisenhower's Federal Aid Highway Act, the result of which was a nation criss-crossed with superhighways. The entire nation was thrown open to commerce on eighteen wheels, and the trucking in-dustry soon became a powerful economic force in its own right: By 1996 it employed 9.5 million people and generated more than $360 billion in annual gross revenue.

Ninety-four percent of today's truckers are men; average age, about forty. An increase in female drivers has been limited largely because long stretches on the road render child care arrangements nearly impossible; many of the new women truckers are empty nesters who join their husbands to drive as a team. But this is no carefree road trip to retirement. From the day you obtain your commercial driver's license, you will remain in constant contact with the authorities. Dave Sweetman carries a three-ring binder filled with an array of permits and fuel-tax forms. Gas tax reciprocity varies from state to state; if you cross a state without buying fuel, you must still pay tax on the fuel you used to cross the state. Get caught overweight, overheight, overwidth, or with the wrong light out and you'll find yourself fined and grounded. Every trucker is required by the federal government to log his activity in fifteen-minute increments; computerization, satellite tracking and in-cab monitoring (right down to engine revolutions) is spreading, and while many truckers welcome the simplification, nearly all of them bristle at the idea of some far-off spy in a cubicle tracking every gear they grind.

Today's trucks are wired. In addition to his steering wheel, Dave Sweetman overlooks an array of nineteen knobs and twenty-five gauges. He can summon up screen after screen of performance data. As we course over the ruts and grooves, the easy lurch of the road reaches the seat through the air-ride shocks, and I am reminded of a trucker in Alaska who once told me his cluster of computerized doodads gave him good information, "but ninety percent of it you feel in your ass."

. . .

Speaking of which, trucking is not good for your hemor-
rhoids. Or your back. Or your knees. Or your anatomy in
general. If your back doesn't go out after years of jostling by
the road, it'll go one day when you're busting your hump to
unload eighty pallets of meat before someone poaches your
next load, or you'll do your knee jumping off a flatbed, or
dropping from the cab. The endless miles set up a craving for
coffee and nicotine, and the fats and carbohydrates waiting at
every diner set your heart and arteries on twin trajectories
eventually intersecting at a stroke.

So much for the body. What about the soul? Truckers will
tell you trucking is frequently twinned with loneliness, that if
you've got trouble at home, the road gives you time and space
to turn it over and over, roll it like a worry wheel, and sometimes you run it down, get it corralled, but more often than
not it just wears a deeper groove. Loneliness and distance create their own little market for companionship. At the Nevada
line, a warm-voiced woman offers a brief, polite invite over
CB channel 19: free hot coffee and free hot showers, available
at a place just off the road; additional services, available for a
fee. Many trucks sport decals in the image of a reptile
stamped with a red circle and slash, meaning the driver is not
interested in the services of freelance hookers truckers call
"lot lizards."

. . .

I switch trucks, riding out of Iowa and into Nebraska with
Bandit and his wife, Lady Frog. They're pulling two backhoes
on a flatbed. Bandit has been assigned to handle public relations for Share America on CB channel 19, the traditional
trucker's virtual hangout. Some good ol' boy calls in, apparently unimpressed: "That convoy stuff, that's a crock a shit."
Bandit keys up the mic. "Well, I'm sorry you feel that way,
sir," he says, his voice like a wood rasp drawn through steel
wool. "We're just trying to improve the image of trucking
and encourage everyone to make that little extra effort to
make our highways and byways safe—if that ain't for you,
well, have a safe trip, driver. This is the Bandit, and we're
outta sight."

Bandit lights a cigarette. "I smoke too much." He's small
but stocky. Ex-military. Loaded with turquoise jewelry. He
does smoke too much. His laugh sounds like melted cheese.
But he maintains that measured military bearing, a stance that
suggests sudden moves are ill-advised. I'm perched in the
bunk, and he looks at me in the mirror. "You want something
to drink? The fridge is right there. Please—you are at home.
Anything." This is a new Freightliner Century. Capacious.
You can stand up in the sleeper and still not reach the skylight.
The refrigerator is studded with novelty magnets: a Snoopy, a
pineapple, a banana, a watermelon, strawberries, grapes, one
in the shape of a tooth, several shaped like states. A counter-
top holds an array of scented candles—one placed atop a

doily—a stock of vitamins, and a flowered box of Scotties tissues. A tapestry of a semi superimposed on the American flag hangs over the bunk, which is loaded with embroidered pillows and stuffed animals. The Trucker's Prayer is clipped to Bandit's sun visor. A solid crucifix is centered over the windshield. This is not a truck. This is a home, a business, a shrine.

I ride with as many truckers as I can: Jim, originally from Frog Jump, Tennessee, who bounced my kidneys across Nevada in a Wal-Mart truck filled with giant orange jack-o'-lantern leaf bags. He has a part-time gig as an Otis impersonator for *Mayberry R.F.D.* conventions. Lee, sixty-seven, running freight with his wife of forty-six years, listening to twenty-five hundred watts of Pink Floyd and Ravel, stopping at schools to give truck-safety seminars. George, his gorgeous canary-yellow Freightliner Classic grossing eighty thousand pounds, loaded with Hidden Valley dressing and Armor All. He loves the road, but misses his two babies and wife back in New Jersey; and, with another baby on the way, he thinks he'll trade the Classic in for a wrecker so he can work close to home. George is training a rookie, Marques, and as we roll under the sun in Wyoming, he tells Marques it takes twice the woman to be a truck driver's wife than it takes a man to be a trucker. The Connecticut Yankee, an ex-policeman loaded with cardboard. He used to drive local, in Long Island. Hated the bumper-to-bumper madness. He waves at the big western sky. "This is like vacation every day." He blames trucking's image troubles on "Billy Big Rigger; the guy who trashes around the truck stop playing video games for two hours, then hammers down the highway trying to make up for lost time." And then there was Thurley, the woman who trucked me in a smaller rig across a numbing stretch of Nebraska. Thurley simply bustles with goodness. "Look at that, look at that!" she kept saying, pointing at yet another wearying flat-line vista. "Praise the Lord. Thank you, Jesus." She thanked the Lord every quarter mile. Look, I wanted to say, this really isn't His best work. But that's my problem, not hers.

On the convoy's last night together, we gather in a casino parking lot just inside the Nevada state line. It's a jolly little carnival. Joey Holiday, a singer who does a truck stop tour and bills himself as "The Nation's #1 Trucker Entertainer," unfolds his tiny portable stage, and sings "She ain't just a truck, Lord, she's my best friend." In between songs he emcees a coin toss to raise money for a child's wheelchair. Above us, the casino marquee—an exploding neon rainbow—grows brighter as the night grows darker. Jim comes out in his Otis clothes, does a ten-minute improv around the fact that he's been driving for two days with a splinter in his butt. The truckers eat it up, guffawing and shaking their heads. I recall these faces a few weeks later when I come across a Salon.com piece in which the writer takes a sarcastic jab at "—those American Trucking Association propaganda films they used to show to high school civics classes. 'Did you know that the clothes in your closet and the food on your table were delivered by truck? That's right. Think about that the next time you see a trucker—and give him a friendly wave!' "

The ATA is hardly impartial, and the road has its share of dangerous, unfriendly truckers. While industry representatives are quick to point out that the number of deadly accidents per mile are down (and have been decreasing steadily since 1982), there are still enough large trucks (4,871 in 1997) involved in fatal crashes to keep groups like Citizens for Reliable and Safe Highways (CRASH) actively lobbying for further restrictions. But: Did you know that the clothes in your closet and the food on your table were delivered by truck? The *Without Trucks, America Stops* slogan is unsophisticated, but we're all complicit in that premise, every single shopping one of us. It is simply not feasible to run train tracks to every grocery store and Wal-Mart in America. Air drops are imprecise and messy, and canals are out of the question. Dave and Bandit and Thurley are on the road to feed our collective habit. We voted them there with our wants and charge cards. Little wonder, then, that they are troubled by our casting them as the heavies.

· · ·

Tomorrow I will roll into Reno with Dave Sweetman, and his odometer will kick over two thousand miles on the nose, just like he said, and we'll all gather up at the Knights of the Road Truckerfest before embarking on an air horn–blasting parade through downtown Reno. But tonight we're all just hanging out in a parking lot, happy to be truckers. And one hundred yards to the north, out on I-80, the economy rolls on.

1999

Rolling Thunder

In 1988, a small group of Vietnam veterans rode their motorcycles through Washington, D.C., to protest the U.S. government's abandonment of prisoners of war and soldiers missing in action. Since then, the protest—known as Rolling Thunder, in reference to the sound of the bikes and the massive bombing campaign carried out during the Vietnam War—has grown to include over 270,000 participants.

◌ ◌ ◌

Midnight at the the Wall. We enter on an incline, descend past the first thin sliver of names, then edge silently downward to the darkened vertex, the incline running deeper and the sliver widening until the names stretch beyond the reach of a tall man. A smattering of candles flutter along the footpath and set the polished Bangalore marble to gleaming like sheets of black ice. But if you lean in close and turn your head, as if listening for the names, you'll see the candlelight caught in a film of fingerprints. The satin marble face—cool and smooth as lacquer—invites touch. Few people are drawn to the Wall without being drawn to touch it, and the prints are trace elements of this instinctive ritual.

But then your fingertips come to rest on a sandpapery row of etched letters. The letters form a name. You think of the mother then, cradling the baby, speaking that name. Then you conjure a young man's face to match. The image is necessarily incomplete, necessarily ghostly. And then you find yourself wondering what you might have been doing that day in '59, or '68, or '75 when—still young—he fell. The power of the Wall is in those names—a silent roll call grit-blasted into the stone to remind us that we are not honoring an abstraction, we are honoring 58,214 comrades; each with a life, each with a death. Each with a name.

But there are names missing. And so early the next morning, after four hours of sleep, here I am on the tail of an Eighty-fifth Anniversary Edition Harley-Davidson driven by a sharpshooting ex-marine everyone calls Murdoch, wind slapping at my ears, rolling up Interstate 66 toward Washington, D.C. The sun is risen and the land is green, but it's early, and the cold air stiffens my knuckles. A staggered double line of dancing headlights trails us in the mirror. And running right behind them, looming like the mother ship, is a big black Class 8 Volvo semi tractor. Most of the guys in this motorcade had a hand in building that Volvo as part of UAW Local 2069, and they've brought it with them to help honor the names you don't see on the Wall, the prisoners of war and missing-in-action soldiers who never came home.

By 7:45 a.m. we pull into a fifty-eight-acre parking lot outside the Pentagon. There are already several thousand bikes in line. It'll be a noisy day. Then I think of the names on the Wall, and the names not on the Wall, and I think, well, it *oughta* be noisy.

The bikes — Harleys, mostly—roll in for hours, in fits and starts at first, but then in a steady, rumbling stream. By 11 a.m., the overpass leading to the parking lot is swarmed with spectators; like a gaggle of flightless birds, they perch chockablock on the railing, flock the sidewalks and spill down the grassy slope overlooking the swelling sea of cycles below. The bikes are packed cheek by jowl, clicking and cooling, canted on their kickstands in ranks roughly ten abreast. Riders milling around on foot lend the scene a sort of constant motion. They check out each other's bikes, snap pictures, reunite with friends. There are a lot of bare arms, a lot of tattoos. A group of eight riders who look like a bad stretch of highway are holding hands and leading each other in prayer. Artie Muller, Rolling Thunder's founder, stands alone in the center of a clear spot, surrounded by lights, cameras and satellite gear, all rigged up in a C-SPAN headset, answering questions none of us can hear. It's overcast now, but warmer. The bikes keep coming.

At high noon a cluster of red, white and blue balloons rises into the air and the parking lot begins to rumble. Beneath me, the seat shudders as Murdoch fires up the Harley. One row over, a long, tall biker with skin to match his leathers pogos up and down on the kick starter of his chopper, a rough hunk of work that looks more like a plumbing project than a motorcycle. He runs out of breath and a buddy strides over to help him. The buddy is heavier, and when he brings his full weight down on the kick bar, the bike backfires, then chugs to life. For a while, while we wait to get moving, the exhaust becomes a little overpowering, but everyone is too keyed up to care.

When we finally swing out toward Arlington Memorial Bridge, and I catch my first glimpse of the spectators, I feel a thrill. And when Murdoch snaps off a salute to a solitary middle-aged Ranger standing at ramrod attention, the thrill turns to tightness in my throat. I get that feeling all along the route.

We swing right at the Lincoln Memorial, rumble up Independence Avenue, hang a left around the Capitol and cruise the home stretch down Constitution Avenue. I remember the trip in glimpses: the family, curbside, holding a homemade sign: *Where is Private Jack Smith?* Clenched fists, raised alongside peace signs. Murdoch exchanging "Hooah!s" with grinning marines. Kids with flags. A man in fatigues, with a quiet face, just watching. Murdoch rapping the engine, and the echoes splattering back from the government buildings. The smell of overheating engines, hot clutches.

And then it's over. National Park Service police on horses direct us onto the grass of the Mall. Murdoch and I leave the bike, double back and catch a ride on the back of the Volvo. Then we end up sitting in the grass beneath a tree. I remark on the irony of so many Vietnam vets being here, on the very ground where their actions were so vehemently opposed. The protested have become the protesters. He agrees, but points out that many of the original protesters show up to support Rolling Thunder. "They realize the soldiers did what they were told," he says. "They were called, and they went."

In this age of declining postmodern irony, it is fashionable to dismiss such loyalty as gullible foolishness or blind jingoism. But to do so is to deny a cold truth: Vietnam may have been a mistake, but the loyalty of the troops misused there still underpins our very existence. The time will come when it is required again, and if you have grown used to freedom, you better pray someone is still willing to risk theirs for yours. Like it or not, deny it or dismiss it, eventually you need someone willing to do a little dirty work in defense of the ivory tower and the well-groomed suburb. Murdoch and I talk a long time, then walk to the Wall. The bikes are still rolling across the Memorial Bridge.

On Monday, a few of us returned to the Wall for a memorial service. The speakers on the dais were joined by an empty chair draped with a pair of fatigues, a helmet, and a set of boots. It was a reverent coda to the previous day's thunderous remembrance.

When I got back home, I tried to describe the thunder of 270,000 motorcycles, the passion in the peace signs and fists and salutes, and the desolate power of the names, and the empty boots. Mostly people were polite, but their eyes took on that wary glaze we reserve for street preachers and prose-lytizing relatives, and I had just the faintest taste of what it must have been like to return from the jungle in '68 and search for a sympathetic ear.

When you face the Wall at midnight, the Washington Monument is all lit up at your back, standing clean as a butcher's bone and solid as a compass pointing the way to Glory. It is a monument to look up to, a monument to remind you of all this country ever hoped to be. The Wall, on the other hand, is cut darkly into the earth. To see the Wall, you have to hunker down and peer into the marble until you find your own face looking out, strung with names.

1998

☼ ☼ ☼

P.S. In *All Quiet on the Western Front*, Kropp proposed that wars be resolved by having the leaders dress in swimming trunks and beat each other with clubs. It does not happen, and we find ourselves back on the overpass, waving at our neighbors as they depart on our behalf.

The Road Gang

Note to non-truckers: The line "Ten forward gears and a Georgia overdrive" comes from the classic Dave Dudley song "Six Days on the Road." To save fuel and gain speed coming down hills, old-school truckers used to shift their trucks to neutral, otherwise referred to as "Georgia overdrive."

❁ ❁ ❁

The road, at night. Thirty miles up in the rare cold black, the ionosphere bounces madness back upon the earth. Waves of amplitude modulation yo-yo from the sky, hopscotching squares of latitude and longitude. Roll the AM tuner and the dial winds through a netherworld; a pulsing, electrostatic ebb and swell of fuzz and flash. The ephemeral spirits in the machine spout prophecy and damnation, provide news without context, dawdle through the late innings of a White Sox game. Dante trips out with Marconi, and their nocturnal spawn dance the dash, dive through your head, chase you down no matter which way you travel.

The phrase "nocturnal spawn" would likely put Dave Nemo off his biscuits. He's an unassuming man, with a light, friendly tone. Put himself through college in New Orleans, on the barges and in the bars, pulling tow and playing country music. Got a part-time job at WWL in New Orleans, but it was 1969, his lottery number was 17, and Uncle Sam was still taking. Wound up in Korea, on the overnight with Armed Forces Radio. A year and a half passed, and he was back at WWL, broadcasting country music for truckers on a new all-night radio show they were calling the Road Gang. Twenty-five years later, he's still sending out skip, now from a tiny bunker of a studio a rock toss from the Country Music Hall of Fame in Nashville. And the members of the hall would approve. In the gold-plated era of radio consultants and computerized playlists, Nemo works with a box of recipe cards and has gone toe-to-toe with guys in ties. Radio is no business for a purist, and yes, Shania Twain commands a card. But the bulk of the names penciled in the mix run to the likes of Cash and Cline, Haggard and Jones, Williams and Wynette. You can still hear Lacy J. Dalton on the Road Gang, or a teen-aged Tanya Tucker, or Tommy Collins—the man Merle Haggard called Leonard. Dale Watson is big with the truckers, and up until they caught the wave, BR5-49 used to drop by and pick a few on their way home from Robert's Western Wear. If you drive all night, you'll hear a pair of fifteen-minute Road Gang Hammer Down Bluegrass Breakdowns. Nemo keeps a banjo under his bed; sometimes he grins and says if he had his way, the Road Gang would be all bluegrass, all the time.

The legendary American trucker isn't the hero he used to be. Clueless renegades, bad press and an ignorant public have all taken some of the shine from the stacks. Automakers love to tout their air bags and V-6 snap in the looming shadow of Tyrannosauric trucks. A van slides into the oncoming lane, and the *St. Louis Post-Dispatch* reads "5 Killed As Tractor-Trailer Hits Van." Some yobbo in a bitsy four-wheeler sees a ten-foot patch of concrete off the front bumper of a Kenworth and homesteads it in a heartbeat. And last week's behemoth Mid-America Truck Show in Louisville was salted with the occasional log-book-bending *Deliverance* extra. But the bottom line is this: Taken as a whole, the best drivers on the road—men and women—are still truckers. Shut 'em down, and the negative buzz will be obliterated by pampered howls of deprivation. On the Road Gang, truckin' songs are received without irony.

You'll hear truckers on the show. They are their own sort of skip, their lo-fi voices ranging the Rand McNally plat. Night Train is on the line. He has his landing gear down and will sleep at home tonight. Bowlegged Snake checks in. Half Breed, T-Trucker, Six Pack, King Korn, Gatekeeper, they all make contact. Cherokee is in Fort Smith, headed to Pennsylvania. The Denver Dreamer is rolling through Denver. Jeff, no handle, no truck, isn't going anywhere—he's calling from an oil platform in the Gulf of Mexico.

The writing life took me to the Mid-America show last week. It was a good gig. Met the guys who haul the Budweiser Clydesdales. Helped Reba McEntire's truckers load out twelve semi trucks' worth of stage, rigging and electrical tinsel. Took three days and sifted through about twenty-five acres of trucks and all things big rig. Come Saturday afternoon, I pulled out for home. Glanced at the map, slipped inside the blue vein of I-65, and rolled north out of Louisville. By the time I hit the Wisconsin line, I still had three hours to go. I kept the Road Gang tuned, punching between WWL and WLAC. Kevin Gaskin, Ol' Spiderbite, was covering for Nemo. He wished it was warmer, so he could go catfishing. Fugitive called from Albuquerque to talk about Hale-Bopp and remind everyone to watch for the eclipse. Pinkard & Bowden filled the "Trucker's Chuckle" slot. In NASCAR news, as always, the names were the same, but they said Earnhardt was struggling. Chaplain Joe Hunter checked in with Truck Stop Ministries to help Mr. and Mrs. Trucker down Heaven's Road. And between it all, the music: Johnny Paycheck. Jerry Reed. Roger Miller. Joe Stampley sang "She's Long-Legged," with a straight face. I was just home when Ol' Spiderbite pulled a new one from the recipe cards, something by a guy named Jack Ingram.

There are other trucking radio shows. The Truckin' Bozo,

out of WLW in Louisiana; Marcia Campbell and Jerry Min-shall, with Interstate Radio Network. Bill Mack has been on the air for years. Wrote "Blue" for Patsy Cline; a girl named LeAnn Rimes recorded it a while later. But I heard Dave Nemo first, at 2 a.m., somewhere in the middle of North Dakota. And so, out of loyalty, when I'm on the road for the overnight, I drive as if my barnacled 1989 Tempo has ten forward gears and a Georgia overdrive, usher in the skip, and collect my mile markers with the Road Gang.

1997

☐ ☐ ☐

P.S. You can still catch overnight trucking shows on the radio (I was listening to the Truckin' Bozo just the other night), but there have been many changes in the names and programs since this piece was written. Today's Truckin' Bozo is actually Son of Bozo. For his part, Dave Nemo now broadcasts exclusively on satellite radio. No more AM skip. I hope it's working out. He was always nice to me. If I was rolling through Nashville after midnight, I'd buzz the studio door, and he'd let me in to shoot the breeze and talk to the truckers on the air. These days my favorite late-night AM skip comes out of St. Louis—the John Carney show on KMOX. Carney is at 1120 on the dial. As they say, that boy ain't right.

Fear This

My fear is my substance, and probably the
best part of me.

—*Franz Kafka*

I don't get to town much, so being cut off
in traffic should have been a novelty. A stream
of bumper-to-bumper day-jobbers droning
homeward, doing sixty in a forty-five, light
turning red 200 yards ahead, and this non-
signaling knothead shoots in front of me like
he's going for the pole at Daytona. Pinches
himself between me and some four-door, and
then stomps the brakes like he's smashing a rat.
And so I sat behind him, wondering if I had
time to rip out his valve stems before the light
changed. His baseball cap was on backward, of
course, his stereo—as I am confident he would
have put it—was "cranked," and he was driving

one of those yappy little four-wheel drive pickups that have become the toy poodles of the truck world. But while all of these things triggered my pique, it was the "No Fear" sticker in his rear window that sustains my rant.

The "No Fear" logo represents a line of clothing and sports gear. Irksomely ubiquitous on windshields, t-shirts, caps, billboards and bumper stickers, this bellicose bit of marketing has caused me to ponder what I know of fear. Very little, I suspect. Not because I am immune, or brave, or drive a hot little truck, but because of good fortune, and because what fear I have experienced—in the face of a well-armed Hungarian border guard, in the back of a fire engine, down a Belize City back street—has been, in the scope of things, fairly superficial. But in today's society, where rebellion amounts to a nipple ring, a Kool-Aid rinse, or an exquisite tattoo, superficial covers it. Image—be it ephemeral as a cathode ray and thin as ink on a two-syllable bumper sticker—while it is so obviously nothing, is, in the age of identity purchased at retail, everything indeed. And every marketer believes—that is not to say they understand—the words of French playwright Jean Anouilh: "An ugly sight, a man who is afraid." Fear is ugly, and ugly doesn't sell sunglasses.

But what sort of vacuous buffoonery allows us to adopt such slogans? Consider the case of the lump of gristle with a pulse who cut me off in traffic. Cossetted in a society where rebellion has been co-opted by commerce, where individuality is glorified in fashion campaigns that put youth in world-

wide lockstep with an efficiency despots only dream of (assuming, of course, that the people who own athletic shoe
companies are not despots), raging youth finds itself sitting at
a red light, steeped in the same hormonal invincibility that fu-
els ravaging armies, with nothing to do but wait to tromp the
accelerator of a trendy little pickup. Who knows fear?

I once hitchhiked a ride with a Belizian cane hauler. I
couldn't speak Spanish; he couldn't speak English. It didn't
matter: The bellowing engine precluded conversation. We
simply grinned at each other as he hurled the truck through
the twists in the road, the scorched sugar cane swaying high
above our heads. The truck was of indeterminate vintage. The
play in the steering was such that an entire half spin of the
wheel was required before the truck's vector was affected.
The previous evening, on a blind corner, a pickup had veered
over the center line, crashing head-on with a tractor hauling
cane. Two men had been killed. As we shot the same curve
that morning, the wreckage still remained; grieving clusters
of family stood along the roadside. We hit that curve full tilt,
blowing a backwash of cane leaves over the upended tractor. I
sneaked a peek at the speedometer. It was completely ob-
scured by a circular decal of the Virgin Mary. We grinned at
each other again.

Two men, both driving dangerously in trucks, both ex-
pressing themselves through adhesive symbology. And yet
there is a difference; an instructive distinction.

Is the cane hauler wiser because he knows fear? Poverty,

dangerous labor, the hungry faces of a brood at home—surely these cultivate acquaintance with fear. The Virgin Mary decal seems evidence of theistic fear. But these are presumptive conclusions, and, I think, just miss the point. That point being, if the cane hauler drives without fear it is because he has acknowledged fear, and then turned it over to the Blessed Virgin. The fellow in the four-wheel poodle, on the other hand, is fearless because he has never been forced through circumstance to acknowledge fear's existence. He has made the quintessentially American mistake of thinking his life is special, his bumper sticker is bold, his truck is shiny . . . because *he* is special. His fearlessness is an inane statement construed through an accident of birth. In contrast, the cane hauler may dispense with fear, but he knows better than to scoff at it.

Ernest Hemingway wrote about people living "essential, dangerous lives." Those three words say so much about what we are or aren't, and explain why, in a world filled with fear, we would choose to disguise the sheltered nature of our existence through mindless sloganizing. Perhaps the pickup driver could back up his bravado; swagger through a Rwandan refugee camp, exhort those pitiful laggards to get a set of decent basketball shoes, hoist a microbrew, and shake off this unattractive predilection to fear. Tell 'em this is Planet Reebok, and on Planet Reebok, we have no room for the fearful. Better yet, he could earn his No Fear decal by strapping on his favorite Nikes and sprinting down Sniper Alley beside a twelve-year-old Sarajevan on a water run. Somehow, after that, I think he'd prefer to keep his rear window clear, the better to see what fearful thing might be creeping up on him.

1997

End of the Line for a Depot Man

Everybody's got a Greyhound story. You haven't really yanked the slack out of the Great American Road Trip until you've gone Greyhound. And you *will* wind up with a story. The Grey Dog is every country music song ever written, on wheels. It's a rolling Coen Brothers film with casting by John Waters.

Ray Grams has a Greyhound story. It stretches over thirty-six years. Funny thing is, Ray never left town.

"March 22, 1965." Ray will tell you to the day when the story began. He came to Eau Claire, Wisconsin, a young man in his twenties, and took over the old bus station. He learned the ropes, selling tickets and checking bags, and one year later—"March 22, 1966," says Ray, exactly—he moved into a new depot a block away on South Farwell, the main drag through downtown Eau Claire. The depot was built to Greyhound specs, a squat box of tan bricks and blue trim, with a steel lean-to foyer.

For the next thirty-five years, Ray was as much a fixture as the bricks. He worked behind the counter, swept the floor, cleaned the restrooms, and hauled luggage, presiding over other people's journeys. At the end of each month, he tallied the numbers for the home office in Dallas and geared up to do it all again.

All those pilgrims—runaways and returners, comers and goers, inbound and outbound, with Ray a part of their journey, but Ray never moving. "I was there for thirty-six years, and I don't believe I ever left town on a holiday," says Ray. "Relatives would want to visit, and my wife would welcome them, but she'd say, 'Ray will probably be working—not all day every day, but he'll be down there at least a few hours.'" Ray is in his living room, watching Notre Dame football. He turns the sound down to tell the story. On July 31, 2000, the bus station closed for good. Ray puts it this way: "I pulled the pin."

Greyhound has had some good years lately. Total revenues are up, earnings are up, and ridership is up. Greyhound's parent company, Laidlaw, is struggling and has stopped supplying working capital, but Greyhound still puts three thousand buses on the road, making twenty-two thousand North American departures daily. Greyhound says 19.4 million passengers took the bus last year, up 6.6 million from 1994.

But for Ray Grams, things have been getting tight, and he reckons his depot won't be the last to close. Nationwide, there are roughly 1,800 places to catch a Greyhound. Of these, approximately 1,650 are run by commissioned agents. "If I didn't sell a ticket, I didn't make any money," says Grams. "You can now buy tickets on the Internet. And before, they never had a 1-800 number. Now, if you're not going to travel for at least ten days they'll take your credit card and mail your ticket, and then you'll come into the station and say here's my ticket, please check all my baggage—well, we do all that for nothing.

"You've got the lights on, and the heat on, and the air conditioning when it's needed, and if you're not making any money, you can't afford to pay the bills. I think that is going to be the demise of the small-town bus depots." He speaks matter-of-factly, without bitterness. "The only way to change that is if they start paying a percentage based on the number of people boarding at the station."

The local newspaper quoted Ray in a brief piece marking his retirement. "I will definitely miss it," he told the reporter. "When you deal with the public for that long a time, you miss it."

Have you done much time in Greyhound stations? Can Ray

really mean it? "Oh yes," he says. "I ran across just about any kind of people that you might ever imagine. We ran the gamut, from the most downtrodden to wealthy people who never cared to fly. I've had some where you'd have to finally call the police department, but generally, when you'd have some people there with a layover, you'd have the opportunity to visit, say, with a bunch of grandmothers talking about the grandchildren they're on the way to see, or their daughters or sons. Or the college student on the way to school, frettin' about the test they're gonna have. And also the type of people who'd say, 'Well, I'm on my way to interview for a new job.'"

Even when the stories weren't so happy, Ray felt privy to the drama. "We'd get prepaid ticket orders, say where a trucking company would call and issue a ticket for somebody to go to Albert Lea, Minnesota, or Salt Lake City, or Seattle . . . whether they didn't make the grade as a driver, I don't know—I never got too involved. Sometimes Mom or Dad would come in and pay for a ticket at our office, and we'd notify a depot in whatever city to issue a ticket to a child somewhere that went out on their own and couldn't make it."

He had a few regulars, like the respected businessman from Iowa who'd get to hitting the bottle and wind up afoot in Wisconsin. "He must have known someone here, because they'd come down and buy him a ticket," says Ray. His waiting room was about the size of a living room, and Ray treated it that way.

. . .

Most people who get off the bus in Eau Claire smoke a cigarette and leave. They debark and loaf to the curb and back, trying to shake the feeling that the road has turned their blood to wash water. "We originated an awful lot of riders out of that station," says Ray, "but most of the people are passing through."

The abandoned depot abuts the Eau Claire River, right across from the public library and a stone's throw from the post office. The library is well kept and busy, and a vibrant farmers' market springs up in the parking lot across the street twice a week all summer and fall, but much of downtown is a collection of dated buildings searching for identity and life while everyone is away at the mall sprawl three miles across town.

In part because of the decline, downtown is home to a number of charitable organizations, including the Chippewa Valley Free Clinic, the Interfaith Hospitality Network, the Hope Gospel Mission, the Salvation Army, and the Community Table. Each of these, as well as the Eau Claire County Human Services building, are all a short walk from the old station.

Blunt economics dictate that Greyhound is the transport of choice for a population always near the end of the line regardless of their destination, and now and then Ray would find someone in need, and he could literally point them to help. The new station is located in an out-of-the-way charter bus building up the hill and well removed from the downtown area, with no city bus connection.

The director of the Hope Gospel Mission has claimed that up to 25 percent of the people they helped came from Ray's depot, and Ray recalls giving riders directions to the Salvation Army or Human Services. Ray is a little concerned about what those people will do now. Helping was part of the job. So was tough love. "Churches would call up and say we've got John Doe, and we want to issue them a ticket, will you accept our check? Well yes, I would do that. And mark the ticket non-refundable, of course. Surprising how many people would get a ticket called in and then wonder if they could get the cash for it. Well, no. That was a complete no-no."

Ray remembers when Greyhound's Ameripass would let you travel ninety-nine days for ninety-nine dollars. These days, a sixty-day pass runs you six hundred dollars. But ninety-nine days on a Greyhound? Riding the bus to a ranch job one summer, I struck up a conversation with two young Israeli men. They were traveling from New York City to Los Angeles. To have sex on the beach with California girls, they said. They were anxious, and felt the bus was overdue. In Hanna, Wyoming, I gathered my stuff and took their leave. One of them reached out and took my arm. "We are almost there, no?" I told him he was just over halfway, and he fell to his seat in despair. Greyhound grinds the size of this country into your skull.

Ray says he'd like to see some of it now. He doesn't care to drive and thinks he'll take the bus. "I'd like to go up into Canada," he says. "And then Alaska. And then fly home after I've seen it all."

For now, he's a little bit at loose ends. "I'm just starting to get used to this," he says. "I stayed an extra month down at the depot after it moved, cleaning out. Filled I don't know how many Dumpsters. I was looking through records back to sixty-five." Now the place is stripped and locked, and in the hands of a developer.

But put that Ameripass on hold. Ray says the people at the new depot have called. "It looks like I might go back and work three to four hours a day," he says. "Maybe two days a week. To help those people out."

2000

○ ○ ○

P.S. In *Population 485*, I described my first Greyhound ride. I caught that bus out of Ray's station. Four years after this piece was published, Greyhound cut over 250 small-town stops from its routes.

The Haul Road

Notes for nontruckers: Western Star is the brand name of a Canadian-made semi tractor. The average fully loaded semi running on a smooth concrete highway "grosses" roughly eighty thousand pounds. The term "90-weight" refers to an extremely high viscosity engine oil. The "fifth wheel" is a large steel plate that serves as the point of attachment between the semi tractor and trailer. A "Jake" is a specialized braking device that allows a trucker to throw a switch and essentially make the engine work against itself.

○　○　○

If you stick your rig in the ditch along Alaska's treacherous Haul Road, the word starts traveling before the white leaves your knuckles. For the next two weeks, every trucker you meet is a wise guy. You may stop for a bowl of bean soup at Coldfoot and find a Polaroid of your wayward load tacked to the bulletin board. If the R-rated, irregularly published *Chuck Hole Gazzett* is up and running, you can expect your bad day to be immortalized in headines like ABE OMAR PLOWS SNOW, or A SHOOTING [WESTERN] STAR. But nobody laughs too hard or too long. Because up here, they have a saying about drivers who exit the Haul Road unexpectedly: "There are two types of truckers: Those of you who have, and those of you who will."

Tom McAlpine won't talk about whether he has or hasn't. "That's voodoo." He grins, and changes the subject. McAlpine has been making the run between Fairbanks and the oil fields of Prudhoe Bay since 1978, with a three-year break beginning in 1986, when the oil business tanked. He headed for the lower forty-eight, where he worked on a ranch and ran produce. He refers to it as time he spent "outside." When the oil field action picked up again, he returned to Fairbanks, and he's been running the Haul Road ever since. Officially known as the Dalton Highway, the Haul Road was completed in 1974. It runs alongside the Trans-Alaska Pipeline, terminating at the Arctic Ocean. Its primary purpose is to supply drilling operations in the gigantic Prudhoe Bay oil field, 250 miles north of the Arctic Circle.

The map may say "highway," but down where the rubber meets the road, the Dalton is a skinny four-hundred-mile scar of chuckholes, dust, mud, snowpack and black ice that winds its way up and down through swaths of forbidding pine forests, ragged-edge mountain passes and endless sweeps of tundra.

The head of the Dalton is around eighty-five miles from Fairbanks—the only stretch of what could reasonably be called "highway" on our route. We pulled out of Fairbanks at 10:30 a.m., grossing 101,400, our four-axle trailer loaded with 9,426 gallons of methanol, used in the oil fields to keep drill holes from freezing. Almost as soon as we got started, we pulled off the road to fuel the trucks and ourselves at the Hilltop truck stop, the last full-time services for five-hundred miles. The truck gorged on diesel, and we gorged on hot biscuits slathered in 90-weight gravy, served with fried potatoes on a plate half the size of a fifth wheel. Then we struck out.

As Tom McAlpine puts it, the first 130 miles of the Haul Road are "nothin' but shiftin'." We took many of the hills at fifteen miles per hour, and McAlpine kept up a running commentary: "This one here has caught its fair share of trucks. . . . See there where all those trees are flattened? Buddy of mine went in there a few weeks ago. . . . This one's called Five Mile Hill. . . . I stopped to dig a guy out of a car on this one. . . ." The litany continues: Gobbler's Knob ("Misjudge that one, and you learn to back with your brakes locked!"). Oil Spill Hill. The Roller Coaster. Sand Hill ("This one will eat your lunch"). The Beaver Slide ("Guy lost it here once, jammed it in a low gear and wound the engine up—there were wrist pins and connecting rods all over the road"). For mile after rough mile, the big 600hp Cat in McAlpine's '99 Western Star 4964FX is either chomping up a grade or riding the Jake. We stop atop Two-and-a-Half-Mile Hill and walk around the truck, performing a visual inspection. Up here, the pines are daubed with fat licks of snow, and packed snow has taken much of the roughness from the road. "In the summertime, you stop here to count your tires, see how many you have left," jokes McAlpine.

The nature of the Prudhoe Bay run imposes itself on the trucks and truckers in many ways. McAlpine has to replace the peg on his CB mike with a steel bolt. "The bracket vibrates so much, it saws right through the plastic one," he says. Tires are run at low pressure to extend their life—still, they last only about thirty thousand miles. Once started, engines are rarely shut down; all that idle time adds up to a 3.3 mpg lifetime average. Twin spotlights in the mirror racks are aimed at both ditches to illuminate moose—they like to run the Haul Road when they get tired of fighting deep snow. The intense cold can freeze axles in an instant; McAlpine always puts his truck in motion with a gentle left-to-right swerve, checking in the mirrors to see that all the flourescent orange stripes painted on his trailer wheels are spinning.

Sometimes it's not cold enough. "Zero to ten degrees, that's pretty good truckin'," said McAlpine as we left Fairbanks. But later that night, when we inched up Atigun Pass and over the Brooks Range, the Western Star's exterior thermometer read thirty-three degrees—just the right temperature to turn the snow pack into a water slide.

McAlpine drove on the edge of his seat. We had stopped to chain up before the climb—"Chains decrease the pucker factor," says McAlpine—but it was still a tense ride, waiting for the wheels to slip like someone waiting for a balloon to pop. Tom kept looking in the mirror to check his tires. Tires that run white are getting a good grip on the snow pack. Tires that run black are too warm—they're melting, not gripping, the snow. Our tires were running black, so Tom kept one eye out for traction-giving loose gravel at the edge of the road; at the same time, he has learned to distrust that edge—a sharp shoulder might be nothing more than graded snow.

Any trucker who has run a variety of weather and terrain will tell you the jokers in the Haul Road deck aren't unique. What is unique is how often those jokers come up. For five-hundred miles, the road demands constant attention. There's a gremlin waiting every quarter mile: an icy switchback, a love-crazed caribou, a whiteout, a chuckhole blowout that hangs your snout out over some godforsaken ravine.

One of the old hands, a man who goes by the handle of "Pappy," puts up white steel crosses where anyone has died. It's hardly the "tombstone every mile" that truckin' singer Cowboy Dick Curless sang about, but there are just enough of Pappy's crosses along the way to help you think about family waiting at home and grip that wheel a little more tightly.

Truckers meeting atop narrow Haul Road hills have been known to clip mirrors, but such incidents incite more ribbing than road rage. Out here, a sort of rough-hewn courtesy prevails. Each time we met an oncoming truck, each driver slowed, reducing the amount of gravel in the air. McAlpine's windshield is filled with cracks and stars, almost all of them put there by four-wheelers who don't know the rules (the Dalton Highway was only recently opened to the public).

When a pickup full of oil-field workers catches us crawling up the 9 percent grade of the Beaver Slide, they wait until we're about to crest and then radio us. "Yeah, can we get around ya there?" McAlpine gives them the all clear. "Thank ya!" they radio as they zip past. The same thing happens when we're caught by a reefer running produce. The pass is arranged before it's executed.

Every time we meet a truck, McAlpine greets the driver by name. They update each other on road conditions ahead and behind, maybe rib each other a little, but there's very little yakkety-yakkety. "Down there on the 'outside' the CB is a toy," says McAlpine, "but up here it's a necessity." He likes the fact that he knows everyone on the road, likes knowing that if he gets in a jam, the next truck through will pull over to help. "The old rules still apply up here," he says.

. . .

It was long dark when we hit Coldfoot, the unofficial halfway point of the Prudhoe run. Coldfoot is a lonely little outpost with a restaurant that, depending on staffing, is sometimes self-service. Midway through our bean soup, we were joined by Tom's father, Del. He was running cement and had been playing catch-up all day. He would make the rest of the run with us.

It was a Monday night; on our way out the door, we walked past a handful of truckers watching TV. Many time zones away, the Dallas Cowboys were spanking the Philadelphia Eagles, 34-0. The twin Western Stars were idling in the lot. "Dad doesn't like to have anyone out front of him," laughed Tom, and right on cue, Del poured the cobs to 'er. The big blue cab torqued and bounced, and off he went, his moose spotters punching twin holes through the night.

In general, the Dalton Highway passes through three kinds of terrain: aspen and pine-covered foothills on the Fairbanks end, expanses of tundra on the Prudhoe end and, in between, the grand, upheaved bulk of the Brooks Range. The stark breadth of the land is stunning. "Sometimes out here," says McAlpine, "it's like somebody shut all the lights off, turned the heat down, and went home."

But the desolation is trumped by beauty. "Look at this," he breathes in a voice as awed as a first-timer. We're in the Brooks Range now, running with a view to the valley ahead. The moon is fat and incandescent, cradled between two bleached peaks like a bright bead in a gun sight. Ahead of us, and to both sides, everything glows an electric white. "Sometimes," he says, "it looks like a giant black-light poster."

We heave and lurch through the moonlight, the mountains beginning to flatten into rolling tundra. The Western Star's 306-inch wheelbase takes some of the jolt from the road, which is actually much smoother now that we've reached the point where water trucks have been running, covering pits and ruts with a smooth layer of ice. Occasionally, an ice chunk or a rock will deliver a ringing shot to the frame.

By the time we hit the oil fields, it's 1:30 a.m. and I'm nodding off. Everything is socked in fog. Drilling superstructures, studded with halogen beacons, loom through the haze. Over the CB, we bid good night to Del, who will be unloading at another site. Then we park. As soon as the truck stops, Tom hauls a spill pad from his toolbox and puts it beneath his oil pan—environmental regulations forbid even the tiniest drip of oil on the snow. Then he pokes his head into a portable office and checks the unloading schedule. He's in line to be unloaded and on his way home well before noon. He climbs in his bunk, and I sling my bedroll on the sleeper floor. And then, snug in my sleeping bag, I let that big Cat engine purr me off to the best night's sleep I've had in months.

There are times, out on the tundra, when the mercury slides to forty or fifty below and the wind pushes the flexible delineators flat and puts up a horizontal wall of snow, that McAlpine pulls the rig over and idles for three days. He huddles in his warm little cube of air, eating MREs and waiting for the storm to pass. And there are times—when he's babying a trailer full of methanol up one side of the Brooks Range, wishing he had chained up and waiting for the tires to slip— that the fan on his Cat 600 kicks in, and he flinches like someone set off a cherry bomb in his sleeper.

And then there are those times, on the homeward end of a run, when he rounds yet another curve shouldering out over the pine tops and he sees one of Pappy's white crosses, that he's reminded that you don't run this road; it runs you.

But it's not all bad. As we left Prudhoe Bay the next morning, we saw two signs. One said we had 494 axle-busting miles to go; the other said, DON'T BE GRUMPY. And for all the nasty surprises the Haul Road can spring, Tom McAlpine knows his run holds at least one attraction every trucker dreams of: "Once you get up here," he says, "you've got to go home. It's the end of the road."

1999

Aaron Tippin:
A Holler Full of Trucks

A ways east of Nashville, there's a
holler full of trucks. Eleven of 'em, a rough,
beat-up bunch, faced inward on a semicircle.
At one end of that semicircle is an old wooden
shop. You can read a lot about a man by his
shop. This one is generally organized, but re-
tains the comfortable clutter of use. A worn
stand-up toolbox stands front and center; a
screwdriver handle and a few wrenches pro-
trude from gapped drawers. A torn-down
transfer case rests alongside a homemade strad-
dle pit. There's an old yellow fridge covered in
stickers, a plumb-ugly bench upholstered in
Naugahyde, a tiny, tinny boom box tuned to a
country station, and a pair of dusty fishing
poles. And hung on a hook on one wall, along

with a mess of other things, an old forest-green hard hat. On the side, in scuffed orange letters, it says "98 TIP."

"TIP" is Aaron Tippin, the man who first caught the attention of country music fans in 1991 with the single "You've Got To Stand For Something." Other hits followed—"Workin' Man's Ph.D.," "I Wouldn't Have It Any Other Way" and "My Blue Angel." Since his debut hit, Tippin has produced three gold albums, one platinum album, and is currently on the charts with his fifth and most recent album, *Tool Box*. Not bad. But today we don't spend five minutes talking about music. Aaron Tippin wants to talk about his trucks.

Tippin's trucks aren't museum pieces. He's pulled them out of junkyards, yanked them from the weeds, even spotted a few along America's back roads from the window of his tour bus. But where did it all begin? "I think it was kind of an accident," chuckles Tippin. He points across the clearing where his former bus driver, Smitty, is carving out a pad for a bus garage, moving fill with a red-and-black '74 Ford F750. "First dump truck I had on the place," he says. "It's been a good old truck. But I got it, and I thought, this thing won't hold enough dirt to suit me, so I found that old Mack over there." Tippin nods toward a Mack B42 at the far end of the row. It has a black box, and a cab best described as "yaller." "Bought it over in Dixon, Tennessee. Me and Smitty went out there and got it cranked, got it goin', and away we went. It had dirty old fuel in it—I mean the fuel was like motor oil, and it was still runnin'! But it kept gettin' slower and slower, so we stopped and put a new fuel filter in it, and *Pow!* She took off like a shot.

"That's the funny thing about these old Macks. Generally, if they're sittin', in any condition similar to this, you hook a chain to 'em and in twenty feet, they're runnin'. They wanna live more'n anything I've ever been around." Tippin's eyes are bright. "Now that is a spectacular feelin'. Tuggin' on an ol' truck, seein' that smoke comin' outta the stack, then she cracks, and then *brrooom*, it comes to life, and everybody that's helpin' can't help but dance around and holler a little bit."

Tippin points out a Mack B61 dump truck. "This one's special. I got that from a good friend, Billy Ferguson. Billy did the whole campaign with Patton in World War Two . . . talk about stories! The Ferguson brothers got out of the war, came home and bought a dump truck. And now anybody in Mississippi knows the Ferguson Brothers company. They still run Macks." Next in line is a faded red Mack tractor. "That's an LJ," says Tippin. "I believe it's a forty-seven. The cab is built on a wood frame. It's got a Cummins engine in it, which is unusual for a Mack. They tell me that's one of the first over-the-road trucks built that'd do a hundred mile an hour. Buddy, that's flyin'!" Next to the LJ, a Mack B67 is hooked to a lowboy. "I bought that off a guy in Missouri. It was out there rustin' away. That's an old forty-ton two-axle lowboy. Forty tons on two axles is unheard-of nowadays. I use it to haul my dozer."

The other trucks in the semicircle include a '61 White Mustang inline six-cylinder gas burner with a short dump box, and a pair of Mack H67 cabovers. "I figure I'd like to get me a cabover goin'," says Tippin. "If you're gonna haul equipment in tight places, you're better off with a short wheelbase, and you can see a little better outta that thing, too."

Tippin has been using his trucks (and a small fleet of excavation equipment) to complete several major projects on his farm, including the bus garage, a driveway that winds through the hills like a dusty Cumberland River, a clearing and basement for his new house, and soon, a runway. "In the end, I'd like to restore one or two of 'em," says Tippin, "but until we get done what we need done, they gotta work."

Tippin's love for working trucks was born early. "Six years old, growin' up on the farm, I was too little to carry a bale of hay, so I got the steerin' wheel of the truck. Dad put 'er in gear and she'd idle down through the field at three mile an hour and you just kept 'er straight."

Tippin's father was also a flier, and the youngster fell in love with airplanes. He got a pilot's license and was steering toward a career as a commercial pilot when the 1980s' energy crisis led to his being laid off and grounded his plans. And so, still in his early twenties, Tippin got his CDL. "I pulled for Cooper Motor Lines. Drove a White Road Commander. Then I drove a Jimmy for Carolina Western, haulin' dry freight." Between runs he took up serious bodybuilding and started playing honky-tonks, but the days when he would see his songs in the charts were still years away. So he kept working, accumulating experiences that influence his music to this day.

The bright lights have done little to fade the blue from his collar. When I ask him about the old green hard hat hanging in the shop, his voice drops, becomes almost reverent. "That's my old construction hat. Sure is. That's the real deal." Tippin wore the helmet during years spent welding bridge girders and stainless-steel textile-mill equipment. Nowadays he dons a hard hat to open his shows. "Someone told me I should use my old construction hat, and I said, 'No, that hat ain't for fun. It's for real.'"

This topic brings about a moment of truth: I once wrote in a review that the hard hat reminded me of long-lost novelty act the Village People. I tell Tippin so. It's not a comfortable moment, facing someone you've criticized in print, but after a short pause (seemed long to me), Tippin chuckles. "Yeah, that's why I wear it for one song and then get it off!" But then the grin fades, and he looks me straight in the eye. "I've been whupped and whupped by people who write stories about how corny it is, but obviously, to the crowd, it's not corny. I do 'Workin' Man's Ph.D.,' or 'I Got It Honest,' and they're on their feet. They get it the same way I feel it. That's important to me . . . that's who I'm tryin' to please."

Tippin's CDL is still current and comes in handy when he and his band are on the road. "Buses now have to abide by the same laws as the trucks do, as far as drivin' hours are concerned. Generally if we have an overdrive somewhere, I drive . . . so it depends where we've got to go. If it's California, I've got a leg in it somewhere."

But from farm trucks to tour buses, you can bet he'd rather be jamming a set of old gears. "I always loved the old B trucks," says Tippin. "When I was in excavation, I worked for a guy who had one. It had two shifters . . . you had to *drive* this truck. We meet a lot of drivers when we're on the road, and I guarantee you, if an old B model Mack pulls into a truck stop, every driver there goes and takes a look at it, because . . ." Tippin pauses, nods his camouflage cap toward his half circle of old rubber and steel, ready to rattle to life and lug a load. ". . . Because it's out there still doin' what it was born to do."

1996

III. On Tour

Sara Evans

There is a parking lot, somewhere on
the outskirts of Nashville, where the big buses
show up around midnight. There are no
crowds, no bright lights, just the idling diesel
and the dull glow of streetlights reflected deep
in the polish. Now and then a smaller vehicle
will approach, and a figure—often carrying an
overnight bag and a guitar case—will open the
door and board the bus.

At some point the door closes for the last
time, the diesel swells a little, and the bus
eases out into traffic, headed for the interstate,
a gleaming whale sliding into a river of little
fish. Night after night the buses leave
Nashville, each one loaded with Nashville's
biggest export: country music.

Before she was old enough to go to school

herself, Sara Evans used to stand at the front of the school bus her mom drove, facing backward, singing to the high schoolers. "I would sing 'Delta Dawn' and 'Behind Closed Doors,' and pretty much anything they would request," says Evans. "I was three or four, so I thought they were these huge big people."

These days, the requests she gets are for her own songs. Her most recent album, *Born to Fly,* went million-sale platinum in July. Fans everywhere want to hear her sing. And so, with her band and crew on one bus and her husband and toddler son on another, she takes her music on the road.

Last May, she invited *Road King* along for a look at a life many truckers covet. I caught a ride to that dark parking lot, and when the Sara Evans band bus pulled out of town way early Friday morning, I was aboard.

Day One: Detroit
"Ya Want Some Dirt?"

A tour bus is like a second home to the artists and crew. So that first night, rolling out of Nashville in the dark, I was a little uncomfortable sitting in the lounge, surrounded by people who were rummaging around in the fridge for food, chatting and catching up on what they did Monday and Tuesday. In this business, that's your weekend. The drummer was working on his pool. The guitar player was trying to finish his dining room. The soundman had done some painting. As the conversations spun around me, I felt I had wandered into a family living room.

And so, when the tall man sitting beside me on the long couch leaned over to speak to me, I listened politely. "So—you want some dirt on Sara?" I just stared, not quite sure what to say. He leaned closer, looking at me conspiratorially. "I'm the bass player, and I've got the dirt!" I stammered something about this not being one of those stories, and before I could get too twisted up, the tall man grinned. "I'm Sara's brother." Matt introduced himself and said he and Sara grew up on a farm and raised some sheep. I did too, so we've got some common ground. It helps the conversation move along, and by the time everyone is ready to turn in, I don't feel quite so uncomfortable.

There are twelve bunks on the crew bus. They are located in the middle of the chassis, two three-high stacks on either side of the aisle. I'm on the topmost bunk in the back stack. Bus bunks are not for the claustrophobic. Coffin dimensions, basically. Can't sit up. Sara's brother has to sleep with his knees folded into the aisle. You seal yourself in by pulling closed a heavy accordion curtain. But before long, the diesel gurgle, the gentle pitch and roll and the faint *tunka-tunka* of the road send you off to dream.

Working from Home

The first morning out, I wake up early. Still searching for my sea legs, I weave down the darkened hallway, trying not to bump knees or step on protruding ankles, and let myself into the front lounge. Out the big windows, the interstate pavement and the sky are the same sort of gray.

Sitting alone in the front lounge, I take in the details. Video, CD and DVD players. Satellite television, with a blue screen blinking "Video 1." As in any living room, there are remote controls scattered everywhere. A leather couch runs the length of either side of the front lounge, back to a little breakfast nook on one side, and a sink and coffeemaker on the other. A bathroom, a microwave and a refrigerator are wedged between the lounge and the bunks. I have no idea where we are. I know tonight's concert is in Detroit. Engineer Joe Keiser appears and starts some coffee. He had the bunk below me. He says my bunk is usually empty, but last night it chattered and squeaked at every bump, apparently because of my added weight. He says he spent half the night jamming envelopes between the bunk frame and the wall, and trying to reposition the bunk with his knees. He apologizes.

I tell him I slept through the whole thing. He grins and unsnaps the heavy curtain separating driver Gary Lumpkin from the lounge. "Are we there yet?" Joe jokes, then offers Gary a cup of fresh coffee. We slow down and pull off the interstate to get fuel. At the end of the off-ramp, a plastic placard is stapled to the stop sign. "Work From Home," it says, with a phone number. I smell the coffee, watch the rest of the band and crew emerge, stretching and scavenging for cereal and muffins, and think, well, there's more than one way to work from home.

Canadian Serenade

From my hotel room in Detroit, I can see clear across the river into Canada. Twenty stories down, people in cowboy hats and Harley gear are making their way toward the open-air amphitheater across the street, where Sara Evans will perform this evening. There will be country music in the big city tonight.

Everything starts hours before, when Keiser and soundman Lee Beverly start hauling tubs and crates from the bays beneath the bus. They wheel them down the sidewalk, past security and into the backstage area and unpack the whole works. Everything is labeled with bright green gaffer's tape: SARA EVANS—DRUM RISER. SARA EVANS—KEYBOARDS. SARA EVANS—JUNCTION BOXES. Everything, from drums to the smallest microphone, comes packed neatly in a case. Like LEGO, Tinkertoys and macrame all in one, the whole mess has to be snapped, twisted, woven and plugged into place before the show can begin—and undone when it's over.

The band and crew work steadily. The crowd gathers in the amphitheater below. Hours later, in the dark, when the lights come up on Sara, that crowd roars. And, when she tips her head back and reaches for the big notes in "Born to Fly," her voice rings out over the people, up and up, until it hits the looming glass towers of the Renaissance Center, and the echoes bounce over the city and into the night, some of them coming back to earth over there in Canada.

Day Two: Milwaukee
"How Do I Get Your Job?"

You have a hotel room in each town, but it's mostly so you can grab a shower. As soon as the show ends and the gear is stowed, we're on the road again, headed for Milwaukee. The hotel is a convenience. The bus is home.

I ride shotgun out of Detroit in a big recliner that looks out through the passenger-side windshield. I feel like I'm right out on the front bumper as Gary negotiates tangled traffic and monstrous potholes, driving smoothly through the mess until we finally clear the metro and hit our stride on the super slab.

I stay up late, talking to Gary, and by the time I bid him good night, the rest of the band and crew have gone to bed. Before I head back, I ask if he ever thinks about all that precious cargo back in those bunks. He says yes, but then he points at his chest. "Sometimes I think about what's sittin' here," he says. "I've got a wife and three kids at home."

Sara is performing in Milwaukee as part of the touring George Strait Country Music Festival. The next morning, the parking lot behind the stadium is wall-to-wall with beautiful buses. Everything is shine, shine, shine. Gary has his polish kit out, working on the wheels. Gary and Sara's driver, Noel McFarland, are constantly asked how to get a job like theirs. Like many drivers, Gary was a musician first, playing with a number of Nashville acts. "I started driving bus when I realized I could make as much money in half the time," he says.

Noel was a trucker for twenty years, and most recently was a driver for country star John Michael Montgomery. Grinning, he explains that he took the job with Sara Evans when "John Michael cut back on his touring, but my wife wouldn't let me take a pay cut!" They love their jobs, but are quick to point out that it isn't what you might think. "A lot of truckers tell me they want this job because they love country music, and they think it would be cool to see all the shows," says Noel, "but the last thing Sara wants to do during a show is look out and see me in the front row. My job is to be back at the hotel, sleeping and planning the route to the next city. I've seen drivers who spend their spare time hanging out backstage. They don't last." When Gary finishes with his buffing rag, a runner drives him back to the hotel.

Happy Campers
Back at Miller Park, the crowd is huge and colorful. From the stage, it looks like someone dropped a blanket of confetti over all the seats. The monstrous green roof girders are retracted, and the sun spills in.

Sara and the band are charged by the crowd, and the show rocks and soars. Just offstage, Lee bobs and weaves over his sound board, his fingers dancing across the thicket of slim knobs like a man playing a high-speed game of Battleship! The crowd is out of the seats, dancing and singing choruses, and Sara leaves the stage to a huge roar of appreciation. Somewhere back in the Milwaukee Hilton, Gary and Noel are

sound asleep. They are still asleep while Sara is doing interviews and meeting fans, and they are still asleep when the
band and crew and I play h-o-r-s-e at a basketball hoop set up
back by the porta-potties. We are joined by one of the guys
from BR5-49, and then one of the guys from Lonestar. Lee
Ann Womack tools by in a golf cart. She smiles and waves.
It's like a party.

Eventually Noel and Gary reappear, and we are on our
way to Pittsburgh. The guitarist, Shawn Pennington, and Joe
Keiser are in the back lounge, engaged in their never-ending
video football games. They keep the door shut, but every now
and then you can hear the cries of anguish. Everyone else
climbs in their bunks, but it has been a good day, and it takes
everyone a while to settle. I look down from my bunk and see
most of the curtains still open. People are chatting across, and
up, and down, and I think tonight this bus feels like a night at
camp. Up front, isolated by his heavy curtain, Gary has the
hammer down. He'll be up there at it long after the happy
campers drift off.

Day Three: Pittsburgh
Some Fans Go a Little Far

In Pittsburgh, I visit on the bus with Sara, husband Craig,
and their two-year-old son, Avery. Sara talks about the bene-
fits of having leased her own bus for this tour.

"The band is my family on the road, and I depend on them," she says. "I have to spend time with them, to feel like we are a band and not just 'Me the Artist.' I love to be with everybody, but Avery needs his space, so the main thing we try to do is make the bus a home." She is tired, both from her nonstop schedule and from the fact that, unbeknownst to the fans she is singing for, she has just had four wisdom teeth pulled. "I always thought I wanted to be a singer, but I never wanted to be a career woman. But that is exactly what you are in this business. There's just so much that goes along with this besides that thirty minutes or hour onstage."

In Milwaukee, I had followed Sara as she signed autographs for hours, was hustled to radio appearances and fan events by security crews, met with record label representatives, sat for television interviews, and was stopped every ten feet for autographs. She is deeply grateful for her fans and her success, but sometimes when you're watching from the other side, you realize why stars become withdrawn and cautious. Greeting fan club members in a small room, Sara is pressed by a fan who refuses to move through the line after he gets his autograph. "Remember me?" he says. "I was in the front row in 1998, I was the one that kept asking you to play 'True Lies' but you wouldn't." "I'm sorry," says Sara. "I don't remember." The fan leans in. "Even after all of my e-mails?"

Family by Blood and Music

Pittsburgh is another good venue. Before the show, Sara and the band join hands in a circle backstage. Little Avery joins the circle, watching from his daddy's shoulders. During the show, he sits with a nanny over by the soundboard. Three songs from the end of the show, Sara launches into another of her hits, "I Could Not Ask for More." She moves stage left, and as she sings the chorus, she catches Avery's eye and smiles. And with the sun in the sky, the crowd singing every word, and her family—blood and music—all around her, she doesn't seem to have to stretch to find the right emotion.

Gary and Noel put us safely back in Nashville just after 1 a.m. Monday. The big shiny buses stopped in the dark parking lot, everyone filed off, and we set off for our homes. The two drivers had been the first to report to work, and they were the last to sign off. But they could sleep well. They took the music on the road and they brought the music home. One more Monday–Tuesday weekend, and they'd do it all again.

2001

The Osmotic Elvis

The first thing I remember about Elvis is that he was dead. The news was post-dated, and obtained in oblique fashion, but that, as it turns out, is precisely the point where Elvis and I are concerned. The Elvis I know has almost nothing to do with albums or films and almost everything to do with saturation and assimilation. I never went looking for him, never bought his music, never watched his movies. He filtered down and found me. In all his mutable states—the thin Elvis, the fat Elvis; the army Elvis, the Vegas Elvis; the hero, the has-been—to many of my generation he is simply the osmotic Elvis.

When I learned Elvis was dead, I didn't get the news from the news. I got it from a television commercial. I was visiting a friend, and as we passed through his living room—two thirteen-year-olds headed out for another game of h-o-r-s-e—an announcer was promoting an Elvis tribute show to be held on a local radio station. An image of a man with a microphone appeared on the screen in silhouette. As the spot concluded, the image faded, and the announcer's voice, tremulous with a touch of reverb, called the name three times: "Elvis? . . . Elvis? . . . Elvis?" I remember I thought the spot overwrought. And I remember we went about our basketball untroubled that the King was dead. But the osmosis was under way.

In 1991, profoundly recalcitrant country artist Steve Earle recorded the live album *Shut Up and Die Like an Aviator*. Earle was on a grungy downhill slide at the time, the heroin in his veins approaching a lazy terminal velocity. He would shortly be homeless, then incarcerated. He sang like a man forcing up crushed glass. After several encores, the audience whistled for more, but the show was over. As the audio fades, an announcer intones, "Ladies and gentlemen, Steve Earle has left the building." At first listen, I recognized it immediately for what it was: a postmodern invocation drawn on the departed King of Rock 'n' Roll.

Just lately, I've realized something else: I've never heard that quote in its original context. I am familiar with the lexicon, hip to the meaning, but only in a secondhand sense. But that's the thing about the King: You didn't have to be there to "get" Elvis. He gets you.

The Osmotic Elvis

In June of 1988, Kalamazoo housewife Louise Welling told Pete Cooke of the *Weekly World News* that she saw Elvis in the Burger King. "I'm not an Elvis fan," she said. "I don't have any Elvis records or Elvis books. I'm not into Elvis." But she knew Elvis when she saw him.

I know how she feels. I'm not into Elvis either. Don't have his records, don't have his books. But as the philosophomorical songwriter Mojo Nixon once sang, "Elvis is everywhere." You can't ignore Elvis. He saturates the periphery of our existence. I've never seen the '68 comeback special, but I've seen the commercial for the video, and I've seen the slick magazine ad for the commemorative plate. I know it's hip to respond to the mention of a "velvet Elvis" with an arch grin, but I'm not sure why. When it comes to Elvis, I feel like a man who knows all the punch lines, but never really got the joke.

And therein lies a defining Elvis dilemma: Why does a man who evokes jokiness continue to reign supreme in American cultural lore? If he is such a clown, why is he still King? If a guy like me knows so little about Elvis, why do I have such a *sense* of Elvis? Elvis died debauched, dissolute, and in a humiliating posture. Where dying is a means to mystique, he died poorly, compared, say, to Marilyn Monroe, perhaps his closest iconic equivalent. Elvis did some decaying long before they put him in his grave, and everyone had a chance to watch. But all the ugly details—the grocery list of drugs, the cheeseburgers, the tumble from the toilet—did nothing to stop the spread of Elvis. Mythologizing was outpaced only by merchandising. Both continue apace. The King is dead, but the King still sells, and so, long lives the King. It's difficult to focus a search for the source of this perpetuity. There are, as one Web site currently puts it, A Thousand Points of Elvis.

He wasn't the first rock star. Some say that was Bill Haley, and Little Richard would have something to say about *that*. No, rock 'n' roll was ready and waiting for Elvis. He rode it like the ride it was, but it was moving when he got on, and it moved even faster when he got off. Shoot, some say the rock 'n' roll went out of Elvis as far back as '58, the day his hair hit the floor of an army barbershop. It's an important point: We call Elvis the King of Rock 'n' Roll, but that title alone fails to explain his perennial pervasiveness. In "The Academic Elvis," Simon Frith writes, "his fame was dependent on the new mass media of television, Top 40 radio, the teen magazine, the LP. . . ." It is a valid point, but requires expansion. I was the firstborn grandchild on both sides of the family. My baby scrapbook bulges with stacks of film and copious notations documenting my precocious aptitudes. My brother followed in two years. His scrapbook is well stocked but comparatively slim. A second brother arrived three years later. A few pages into the scrapbook, it is as if he stopped developing. The rest of the pages are empty. Today's latter-born celebrities can command media saturation Colonel Parker could only dream of, but our interest is diluted. Elvis was our mass-media first-born, and we have never kept such a scrapbook since.

But what if you reduce mass media in the equation? Aside from a scratchy 45 of "Heartbreak Hotel," I don't recall hearing Elvis in our house. I suppose I read about him in the paper, but we never had a television, and I know Elvis was dead two years before I had a radio.

Radios were forbidden in our home, but in November of 1979, I discovered one squirreled away in a mysterious slope-roofed closet upstairs in our old farmhouse. I've been able to backtrack the date because when I plugged it in, turned it on, and the tubes warmed, I heard Kermit the Frog, singing his way to #25 on *Kasey Kasem's American Top 40* with "Rainbow Connection."

Long before I heard Kermit, back when I was tiny, my brother and I stood in front of my grandma's fireplace, playing what would one day be called "air guitar" while mouthing along to an LP she had put on for the evening. I must have been particularly animated, because my grandma, then in her late fifties, said, "You move like Elvis Presley!" I didn't even know who Elvis Presley was. And yet, by that time, the moves that had gotten Elvis's pelvis banned in prime time had become de rigueur in rock. As limited as my exposure to music and television was, a little drop of Elvis had trickled down and hit me in the hips.

. . .

The osmotic Elvis is not always obvious. You see someone owning the stage, shaking his pelvis and whatever else, and you'll be excused for saying, oh, Elvis started all that. You'd be wrong—he didn't start it, he popularized it—but you'd be excused. But then you see a man like Townes Van Zandt, a frail alcoholic ephemera out of Austin, Texas, dead this year at fifty-two, teetering on the edge of a stool, singing the troubled, introspective songs that made him a legend but didn't make him happy, and you hear him tell the story of how it was Elvis on TV with his guitar and Cadillacs and girls that made Townes ask his daddy for his first guitar. Suddenly you think, if Elvis started this man—the utter anti-Elvis—what else did he start?

Before Elvis was everywhere, he was everything. He was whatever you needed him to be. The dangerous erotic rocker, the good and loyal GI, the grandiose balladeer, the film star, the nouveau riche hick, the Cadillac philanthropist, the strung-out goofball, the prayerful gospel singer, the bloated post-modern icon. He was a national "local boy does good," he was an archetypical cautionary tale. Here he was in 1956, according to John Shepherd, "eminently successful in flouting the propriety of middle-class sensibilities" with his nationally tele-vised gyrations. There he was in 1971, sideburned cheek by shadowy jowl with none other than Richard Nixon, who pre-sented the most famous addict in America with an enameled shield making him an agent of the Bureau of Narcotics and Dangerous Drugs. The irony hits you like an envelope full of pills. The rebel sold out. Officially, symbolically, and to Richard Nixon no less. Little wonder that two weeks after Elvis died, Lester Bangs wrote, "I see him as being more like the Pentagon, a giant armored institution nobody knows anything about except that its power is legendary."

But this bizarre alignment says as much about Elvis's ability to broaden his audience demographic as the artistic range between "Hound Dog" and "Old Shep." How do you like me now, Elvis always seemed to be saying, and what would you like me to be next? He gave us so many ways to remember him, we couldn't forget him. Even if we missed him the first time around.

The future looks good for Elvis. Things will only get better; his image is bound to improve. The whole postage stamp thing was a good omen. It was a highly official way of saying, well, gosh, I think we've made fun of his collars long enough, let's let him slim down and dump the jumpsuit for some vintage lamé.

Applying the Sinatra corollary, we can assume that were Elvis alive today, he would be consigned to embarking on a Mobius strip of farewell/comeback tours, interrupted at regular intervals by celebrity tribute mawkfests. Instead, he's still the sexy shakin' Hillbilly Cat, legal tender backed by the full faith and power of the United States government. And by God, if there's one thing we love in America, it's eternal youth with a fat wallet.

And then, in the mitigation category, we have become inured to celebrity misbehavior. Elvis and his penchant for panty-clad wrestling girls offended 1950s sensibilities, but the year he died Sid Vicious and the Sex Pistols lurched into America. By October of 1978, Vicious was charged with stabbing his girlfriend to death; four months later, Vicious himself was dead. Shooting one's television suddenly seemed positively quaint.

But one need not pick on punk rockers to define deviancy downward. In the twenty years since Elvis pitched forward to glory, a score of his exploits have been eclipsed by any number of our most favored televangelists. In the end, the fact that Elvis lacked Mick Jagger's metabolism and Keith Richards's liver allowed him to mount a posthumous comeback the Jims—Bakker and Swaggart—can only pray for. And perhaps the academics—frequently loath, embarrassed, or unable to judge him as an artist—will let down their hair and let Elvis climb up the ivory tower. Some recent readings have been redemptive, and there has been a trend toward analyzing Elvis the Performer rather than Elvis the Myth, Elvis the Meretricious Primitive, Elvis the Snacker. Strange as it may seem, it may take the demise of Elvis's original legions of fans to pave the path to complete ensconcement. In his own redemptive work, "The Academic Elvis," Simon Frith suggests that "as arguments about performance and identity begin to inform cultural studies, so *perhaps Presley will at last be taken more seriously than his fans* [italics mine]." From this one can infer all that unstinting, uncritical worship made the woolly-heads nervous. I mean, it's not like you've got entire conventions of Beethoven impersonators.

But of course the impersonators won't go away soon, and the sightings won't stop, and some summer, years from now, you'll be stuck in traffic in a strip-mall chunk of town, and the sun will be unforgiving, and right outside your passenger-door window will be some guy set up on half a service station parking lot, selling velvet in a frame, and five or six of those beauties will feature the King of Rock 'n' Roll.

Whether the academics decide to elevate him or not, low culture will keep Elvis alive. Everything "Elvis" is a tribute. Even the embarrassments: the tick-tock clocks that dance, the Elvis shampoo. If I am wrong, and academe turns on him, all the better. The more vitriolic or condescending the observations, the more they stand tribute to an insatiable need to establish the proper position of the icon, to the power of the icon to evoke.

Do you doubt that Elvis can still evoke? I share my first name with two of the most recognized men in the world: Michael Jackson and Michael Jordan. No one ever makes the association. But if your name is Elvis, you cannot *escape* the association. I have no acquaintances named Elvis, although I can think of a few well-known Elvii: Elvis Grbac, the NFL quarterback; Elvis Costello, the musician; and Elvis Stojko, the champion figure skater. But here's the thing: The first time I heard these names, and the last time I heard them, I thought immediately of Elvis Presley. What other name triggers that instant connection? Adolf, maybe. Jesus, certainly. There was a time, I suppose, when people named their boy Elvis because they liked the name, or they had an uncle Elvis who was dear to the family and got kicked in the head by a mule. But somewhere along the line the boy from Tupelo, Mississippi, stole that name forever, and no one else can ever truly have it for their own. You take that name, you live with a legend. Make no mistake. The legend lives, but the man is gone. I have it on good authority from Nashville reporter and Graceland wake attendee Bill Hance that Elvis is indeed dead ("I done seen him"), and posthumous rehab can only do so much. Julie Baumgold drove that point home with just one backhanded line in a gentle, looping dance of an essay written for *Esquire* in 1995. Describing an all-star musical tribute to Elvis, she wrote, "Tributes can be dangerous things, because sometimes all they prove is that it takes forty performers to not quite recall one Elvis."

But then, who needs Elvis back? Elvis was big, but the trickle-down Elvis is culturally colossal. The feeding frenzy took place decades ago, but the postprandial Elvis is very much in demand.

And forever available.

1997

Clarence "Gatemouth" Brown

Friday, September 14, 2001. At the University of Wisconsin in Madison, twenty thousand people are shoulder to shoulder on the Library Mall, honoring victims of the attacks in New York and Washington. The air is cool, but the sun is high and bright, intensifying all the red, white and blue. A man wielding a tall flag takes bellicose swipes at the sky, and the cops bounce a handful of vociferous protesters, but mostly, solemnity prevails.

A block away, at the base of the student union terrace, the waves on Lake Mendota roll to the breakwater with an easy chug and surge. Sparrows work the terrace for crumbs, their beaks ticking at the concrete, pausing only to flutter from the path of the professional class, which is out jogging over lunch break. The joggers pass in talkative packs, leaving sentence fragments in the air. Today, the fragments are all from the same conversation:

". . . relatives on the plane . . ."

". . . which will help with coalition building . . ."

". . . but the people *we'll* kill won't be the ones . . ."

Up on State Street, the poster kiosks are running heavy to peace rally announcements and reactionary screeds. Somewhere under the new stuff is a poster that says Clarence "Gatemouth" Brown will be playing on University Avenue tonight, at a club called Luther's Blues. It's not going to happen. Gate saw the towers come down in New York City, and he's not getting on any airplanes. Right now he's in Louisiana. On his porch. Keeping peaceful company with a gator.

Clarence "Gatemouth" Brown was seventeen years old in 1941, and on the road, playing music. He was standing on a street corner in Norfolk, Virginia, when someone told him Pearl Harbor was burning. His mother, certain he would be drafted, sent him a letter and told him to come home. They drafted Clarence, but not until '46, when the war was over. He didn't care much for the army. "There was so damn much prejudice . . . segregated barracks and mess halls . . . I couldn't understand how in the hell people could live like that when they were tryin' to save each other. They wouldn't let our boys fly no airplanes . . . it's hard to describe how the black man was treated. Nobody seemed to give a damn."

Gatemouth is seventy-seven years old now, and he has seen his nation attacked a second time. He notices the flags are out again. He's not sure how deep the patriotism runs. "Don't get me wrong now—I feel sorry for what happened to those people. But it's the funniest thing—when things is smooth, nobody likes one another, they hate one another's guts. But when a crisis happens, everybody hugs one another with all this bullshit sympathy. I mean, why can't you have respect and concern for each other before? It's just like Christmas— from January to December, everybody is just on your own. But when that one day comes up . . ."

Born in Vinton, Louisiana, Clarence "Gatemouth" Brown grew up in Orange, Texas, near the Gulf Coast. His father fiddled for friends on the weekends, and at the age of five, Clarence began backing him on guitar. They played a little bit of everything—regional tunes, French traditionals and German polkas. When Gate was ten, his father started him on the fiddle. During World War II, he got work as a drummer.

He broke from the back of the riser to the front one night in 1947 when T-Bone Walker took sick during a show at the Golden Peacock in Houston and stopped playing, mid-song. Clarence jumped onstage, picked up T-Bone's guitar, and ripped into his own "Gatemouth Boogie." In fifteen minutes, as the story goes, the crowd tipped him six hundred dollars.

Club owner Don Robey hired Brown, became his man-

ager, and put him on tour with a twenty-three-piece orches-
tra. Soon he was signed to Hollywood label Aladdin Records.
Dissatisfied with Aladdin's promotional efforts, Robey launched
his own Peacock Records label. Brown had several hits with
Peacock, including his signature "Okie Dokie Stomp."

Drawn to Nashville in the 1960s to take part in a local
R&B television show, Brown recorded a number of country
singles. He spent much of the '70s in Europe, where he
recorded nine albums. He also toured the world on behalf of
the U.S. State Department, taking his American music to lo-
cations ranging from Botswana and Madagascar to the Soviet
Union.

In the late '70s, Brown moved to New Orleans and
teamed up for an MCA album with Roy Clark (1979's *Makin'
Music*). The Clark project led to joint appearances on *Hee Haw*
and *Austin City Limits*. In 1982, his album *Alright Again!*
(Rounder) won a Grammy for Best Traditional Blues Recording, and Gate himself received the W. C. Handy Blues Award
for Instrumentalist of the Year. Eventually, there would be
seven Grammy nominations, nine Handy awards and a Pioneer Award from the R&B Foundation. Brown continued to
tour through the '90s and into the new millennium, with
stops in New Zealand, Australia and Central America, again
on behalf of the U.S. government.

For seventy-two of his seventy-seven years, Brown's career has unfolded over a shifting geography of place and

sound, yielding a body of work nearly impossible to catego-
rize. Read the bios and press clippings and you'll find references to blues, roots, jazz, cajun, calypso, zydeco, bluegrass,
country, funk and swing. Ask Gatemouth, and he'll call it
bayou swamp rock. Or border-type country. Or American
and world music. Or American music, Texas-style. He plays,
and leaves the sorting to others. Someone once said his country licks didn't sound country. "What country you talkin'
about?" asked Gate.

On the heels of two albums driven by big-band Texas
swing—1997's *Gate Swings* (Verve) and 1999's *American Music,
Texas Style* (Blue Thumb)—Brown's new release, *Back to Bogalusa* (Blue Thumb), rides a more laid-back bayou groove. "I
wanted to back down," he says. He brought in a few extra
horns, Mike Loudermilk pitched in on electric and acoustic
guitar, and Sonny Landreth and Cajun accordionist Zachary
Richard sat in on several numbers. Otherwise the tracks were
cut with his regular band: Harold Floyd on bass, Joe Krown
on keyboards, David Peters on drums and Eric Demmer on
saxophone.

They didn't dally in the studio. "I don't take no six months
to do no album!" announces Gatemouth. "What you gonna do
on it for six months?!? I know guys stayin' in the studio two
and three months, workin' on four tunes! That's ridiculous!
For what?!?" He pauses to chuckle. "Took about a week.
Workin' at my own pace."

He concedes he's had to adjust that pace of late. Age, he says, and he's all right with that. "Mm-hmm . . . that's the way it is," he muses. Suddenly, a thought strikes, from left field. "These people my age, gettin' all these face-lifts! What for?"

You wouldn't know where to start, eh, Gate? "Hell no! If that rubber band broke on top of my head, the skin'd fall down and trip ya!" Now he's really laughing.

He will speak out. On the trouble with America: "Look at our jails now. They've got forty percent more blacks in jail than whites, and they're all doin' the same damn thing—messin' up. Society feels like the black is into dope, well that's wrong, because the white's into the dope, too."

On the trouble with other countries: "We help every country we can get out of a bog hole, yet, they don't like us. A lot of 'em are very phony about it. And [now] we'll see what's gonna happen when we need help. Once we help them, it's kiss my butt after that. And that's wrong."

On kids these days: "I try to tell the young people, try and not hurt each other, because if you hurt somebody, it's the same as hurtin' yourself. It's hard to talk to the young people because they're into another thing of their own. That goes for whites and blacks and whatever else out there, because they're rebellin' against society."

On body art: "Look today how they're piercin' their faces all up with holes and puttin' earrings in their tongues and nostrils . . . I mean it's *haaarrible*-lookin', man! I have some friends, their daughter's got more holes in her than a sieve. With rings hangin' in every one. And on the other side of the coin, the blacks, especially 'round New Orleans, puttin' all this cheap gold in their mouth, and keeping their mouth open so you can see it. It's very distasteful to me. I just try to tell them, I think you're ruinin' yourself at the same time. They don't seem to care."

On automotive sound systems: "They get right upside of you and turn them things up, and I got a big heavy 1976 Cadillac Sedan DeVille, and it vibrates that car with all the boomin'. Now how in the hell can they stand it sittin' in their cars?"

On infomercial psychics: "That woman on the television . . . if she's so smart, why can't she go and tell us who killed that baby in Colorado?"

On certain white rock singers: "Howlin' like a cat caught in a hot oven."

On blues singers: "Cryin' about who owes them . . . nobody owes you anything!"

On rap singers: "Lookit these rap singers. I mean . . ."

He stops now. "I see so much wrong, and they ain't nothin' I can do about it. We can talk about it, but that's as far as we can go with it." He sighs. "Yeah, I don't know, this world looks like it's sinkin' fast . . ."

How do you avoid cynicism, then, Mr. Brown?

"Well, for one thing, I stay around my house, mostly!"

He's laughing again.

. . .

If Clarence "Gatemouth" Brown the observer sees a lot of trouble in the world, Clarence "Gatemouth" Brown the performer figures crying in his beer won't fix anything. *Back to Bogalusa* is easy on the soul. Hoyt Garrick wrote the lead-off track, "Folks Back Home," a poignant piece in which a man wanders past "empty cars in the railroad yard/where fast freight used to roll." ("Folks Back Home" is one of five tracks on *Back to Bogalusa*—the others being "Breaux Bridge Rag," "Louisian'," "Bogalusa Boogie Man," and "Dixie Chicken"—that are new versions of tunes previously recorded in the mid-'70s for the Europe-only releases by the Barclay label.)

As Hoyt's lyrics unfold, a picture emerges of a lonely, fallible character, facing life alone. But when Gatemouth sings "Movin' in the right direction/With his head up high/Sometimes it's hard to keep the beat/No matter how hard you try," his vocals convey a combination of weariness and warmth that can only be described as equanimity.

The term "equanimity" sounds like faint praise, but it is not. Equanimity is the only thing that will save you from this world, and it doesn't come easy. Or cheap. And you can't fake it for long. Even when the songs strike a note of warning (Bobby Charles's "It All Comes Back") or express disappointment in one's fellow humans (Charles's "Why Are People Like That" and "Lie No Better" by Delbert McClinton and Gary Nicholson), they are not vindictive. Gate's voice—no longer as brash as it once was, but still supple and rich—suggests that there is no false hope in his world, but neither is there absolute despair. Don't expect much, but don't give up.

Accordingly, when it comes to picking songs, Gatemouth chooses his words carefully. "I'll pick the song that's positive, I'll pick the song that's funny," he says. "I listen to the lyrics."

If he favors a songwriter, it is usually for lyrics. "Bobby [Charles, who wrote "See You Later Alligator" in the 1950s] is a very positive person. He's writing about himself, but he's also writing about other things in life. I always pick some of his. And another fellow that's really great, a dear friend of mine, John Loudermilk out of Nashville. I love his writing, because he's very positive about what he writes. Percy Mayfield, he was a good writer. And Delbert McClinton is pretty good.

"These people I'm mentioning are great writers, but it's hard for them to sell their own stuff today. So I'm the one that can take it out there and sell it. I think I was the chosen one to sell their stuff, and they know that.

"Anyway, if I like a song, and I take it, I'll do something with it. In my own way. When I put myself into it, that makes it not a copy, that makes it almost an original. I don't listen to the music. I listen to the lyrics, because I'm going to put my own music on it on average."

Meaning his fiddle is full and strong on "Louisian'" and "Breaux Bridge Rag." Meaning his guitar thinks it is part of the brass section on "Lie No Better." On "It All Comes Back,"

Gate's guitar commiserates with the singer throughout, the Greek chorus to his vocals. On the instrumentals "Grape Jelly" and "Slap It," the brass and keyboards get their generous turns, but when Gate's guitar comes in, there is no question who is in charge. And yet he does it without histrionics. There is an ease to this album that makes it a joy to hear.

There are lighter moments. Brown wrote "Dangerous Critter" for the gator that lives beneath his porch. And he struts a little in "Bogalusa Boogie Man." But it never gets silly. Clarence thinks there is no shame in acting your age. He feels no need to contort himself to get your attention.

"Some of these guitar players from the past, old guys still out there slidin' across the floor and all that . . . there's a difference between a clown and an artist. If you're going to get up there and cut cartwheels and tear up your face and look stupid, you're not a musician, you're a clown! I sit on my stool, and I stand a little bit, and I sit on my stool, but my music's doin' all the talkin'.

"I may never be what they consider a superstar—whatever that's supposed to be. But my music will tell what I don't have to talk about. Such as being positive about life, not vulgar about life, not talkin' about hate and all that sort of stuff. I just don't like that stuff, man.

"The music will hold its own if it's good. If it's bad, it will flop. We know that." He considers for a moment. "Unless it's got a lot of bucks behind it to make it what it's not. And that's happening. There's a lot of music being put up on the top shelf, if they let it fly itself, it wouldn't go on the bottom shelf.

"You call these people ninety-day wonders."

You could call Clarence Brown a seven-decade wonder. Closing in on eighty, and here he is with an album that is vibrant and engaged. But you think you should get beyond the music and ask him how to live, ask him for some of that cantankerous wisdom. What he says is, "Pay attention! To what's around you, what was behind you, and what's in front of you. Pay attention, and you can avoid a lot of mistakes. I mean, you can't avoid 'em all, but the worst ones you can."

There is no question that generations of musicians have learned important lessons from observing Brown's career. Albert Collins, Frank Zappa, Lonnie Brooks and Eric Clapton include themselves in that number. You wonder how many people have learned important lessons from observing Brown's life. He's ready for that one, with a chuckle. "Well, some of 'em say they've learned, but I'm waitin' to see *when*."

Brown says a bunch of bluegrass players, Ricky Skaggs among them, have asked him to do an album. "I don't know what I'll do," he says. "Sometimes I think on it, sometimes I don't even worry about it. What will be, will be. And someone wants me to do an acoustic album. I don't know, man. I'll wait to the last minute, and I'll say, well, I'm gonna do this kind of album. And that's what I'll do.

"You can worry yourself to death. I've got a good friend, he rehearses four and five hours. I say, 'What you doin' it for?' You're not going to learn a bit more pushin' yourself into something that you can't handle. Rehearsing four or five hours, what for? It don't make you a better musician in the first place. It really don't. It makes you find yourself meetin' yourself on every turn."

My generation is sorting out the events of September 11, not sure yet what they mean for ourselves or our country. We have nothing against which we may measure such a thing. In such times, it helps to put ourselves in the presence of our elders. The wise among them draw on experience preceding and paralleling our own and compose important lessons.

If we will listen.

Sometimes the lessons arrive in direct quotes, sometimes they are oblique. *Back to Bogalusa* is a work of hope, dignity, and humor, delivered without pretension by an artist who is no longer surprised by the foolishness and evil men do, and yet is unwilling to yield the stage to bitterness or despair.

He's back out there touring, supporting the latest installation in a discography that stretches back to the late 1940s. Between gigs, he sits on a porch in Louisiana with his pipe. The porch is built over water, and he can fish from his chair. He knows the gator is down there just beneath him, but it's OK.

"We've got an agreement," says Gate. "You don't eat me, I won't eat you."

Equanimity, you see.

2001

☺ ☺ ☺

P.S. Gatemouth was a treat. The older I get, the more I treasure outspoken elders who exercise the freedom to say what they mean. I was thrilled when he said "Pay attention!" as this echoed the first and last lines of a three-line poem written by one of my mentors, the poet Bruce Taylor. The middle line: *This is everything*. You can save yourself a lot of trouble with a poem like that.

In reviewing pieces for this collection, I noticed I tend to invoke the idea of equanimity on a regular basis. It's a worthy topic, but a fellow gets nervous about the repetition. People who write and speak in public tend to repeat themselves in conversation, in part because they are working out their material, floating it out there to see how it goes over. Bits and concepts tend to improve in the retelling. And some repetition (grafting portions of an essay into a book-length work, for instance) is simply functional. But at some point, you want to avoid the same old mantras. There is the danger that you will go from living the examined life to ending each day on your intellectual porch, yelling, "You kids get off my yard!"

Ramblin' Jack Elliott

To ask Ramblin' Jack Elliott a question is to tug at a snag in a sweater, only to see the yarn unpurl of its own volition, dropping in aimless loops, curling and snaking itself into a variegated fable. Every answer is a folktale. Conversation is an exercise in free association, switchbacks, good-humored evasion, meanders, and box canyons. Ramblin' Jack Elliott does his talking without aid of a compass.

I have him on the phone. "We're gettin' ready to go to Oregon in the Mercedes," he says. He's at his home in rural California. The Mercedes is a '75. He bought it very used and has had trouble with it. ". . . and I left the window open overnight on my side, because I was bein' the passenger, and I was kind of tired of the rain, and it stopped rainin', and I was enjoyin' the fresh air, while Jan was drivin' us home from our town, and so the sheepskin seat cover got totally soaked. So now I got the electric heater out of my motor home, with an extension cord from the house that runs into one of the back windows on the lee side of the car, it's open about two inches to let the wire come in, and I've got this heater on the floor on an upside-down aluminum pot so as to prevent any heat from gettin' in the carpet and settin' fire to the car, and it's aimed up at the seat, from about oh, a foot away from it, from underneath the dashboard on the passenger side, 'cause I couldn't get the damned sheepskin off, it's locked on by the [he adopts a Colonel Klink accent, and begins to yell] Mercedes-Benz headrest, vitch iss heldt in place by two vertical chrome-plated, nine millimeter *shtalks!*"

I haven't asked him a question yet. Already the yarn is coming loose. Ramblin' Jack Elliott, CliffsNotes version: Bob Dylan is Jack Elliott is Woody Guthrie. "He sounds more like me than I do," goes the Woody Guthrie quote. They busked around the country. When Woody's rambles ended in a decade-long terminal hospital stop, Jack took Woody's walk, talk and music back to the road. Returning to Woody's hospital room one day, Jack met a boy named Bob Dylan bedside. Taught him some things. Soon, Dylan was getting more gigs. Sometimes the marquee read "Son of Jack Elliott." Ramblin' Jack Elliott, *Who's Who* version: Jack Kerouac, James Dean, Johnny Cash, Waylon and Willie, Sam Shepard, Jack Nicholson, Rod Stewart, Townes

Van Zandt, Kris Kristofferson, Jackson Browne, Greg Brown, Keith Richards, Allen Ginsberg, Ian Tyson, Robert Duvall, Elton John, Paul McCartney, Bruce Springsteen, Doc Watson. All listed as fans or registered acolytes. Mick Jagger left a Ramblin' Jack show in England and bought his first guitar.

But I'm setting him up like a historical figure. He is very much alive. Very much contemporary. Ramblin' Jack Elliott, recent history version: *South Coast,* Grammy, 1995, Best Traditional Folk Album; *Kerouac's Last Dream*, reissued 1997. And now, *Friends of Mine*, partnering Jack with a telling array: Arlo Guthrie, Peter Rowan, Rosalie Sorrels, Tom Waits, Emmylou Harris, Nanci Griffith, Jerry Jeff Walker, Guy Clark, Bob Weir. On songs written by Joe Ely, Gene Autry, Townes Van Zandt, Jerry Garcia, Merle Travis. And Woody Guthrie and Bob Dylan.

I'm supposed to find out what Jack's got to say about *Friends of Mine*. It's not going to be easy.

Ramblin' Jack Elliott, calling from a hotel in Minneapolis. His voice is tired, all stooped over. He's in the midst of a racking cold. It's late autumn, chill and raining. He wants some fresh air. "But there's this musician-proof window, a suicide-proof window," he grieves. "If you want air you push a button. They charge you for air."

He's in his sixties now. A good age, I suppose, for a folk singer. He's been through the '60s before, hitchhiking,

singing, riding around Woodstock on motorcycles with Bob
Dylan and Joan Baez. But tonight he feels old. His hip is acting
up. His guitar didn't make the trip. His companion, Jan, had
to stay behind. Tonight he'll play the Cedar Cultural Center.

I mention Peterbilts. He brightens.

Later, he crosses the wooden floor of the Cedar Cultural
Center with a slanted amble that bespeaks old injuries, helping himself along with a subtle hike of the elbows. When he
stands backstage, it's usually with his hat in hand, his hips
hitched, his wiry legs planted in a stance amenable to forking
a bronc or straddling the roll of a ship's deck.

At fifteen, Elliott Charles Adnopoz took the subway out
of Brooklyn and joined the rodeo. Tonight, in a ribbed and
bibbed shirt, his neck nestled in a bandana you could nap under, he looks every inch the seasoned hand. Young Master
Adnopoz is lost to legend. In his place, a troubadour.

The word is too grand, too affected, to suit the man, but
the definition is spot-on. From Brooklyn to Britain, from
Woody to Waylon, by horse, by ship, by truck, from the '50s
to the millennium, he has never stopped covering ground.
Singing and moving.

And so now there he is, on the stage of the Cedar Cultural
Center, sound-checking a borrowed guitar, playing to the
folding chairs on a wet night in the state where Bob Dylan was
born.

• • •

An assignment landed me on country singer Marty Stuart's tour bus in Petaluma, California, last year. Someone knocked on the door with a note. *Ramblin' Jack is here, wonders if he can come back.* Name meant nothing to me. I got up to leave. "Oh man, no," said Marty Stuart. "You don't know who Ramblin' Jack is? You've *got* to talk to him. He was Woody's cat!"

Ramblin' Jack boarded the bus, hat in hand. "Man, I got something to show you!" said Marty. He disappeared into the back of the bus. In a little bit, he returned with a videotape. An old dub of *The Johnny Cash Show*. He popped it in, and there was Ramblin' Jack, twenty-some years younger, different glasses, different hat. Elliott scoffed at the hat, but you could see he was delighted with the footage.

Back when Stuart was playing in Cash's band, Elliott joined them for a brief California tour. In addition to singing and playing, he traded off at the wheel of a Peterbilt with a curly haired guy he remembers only as Wirehead. They were hauling Cash's sound equipment. "We got on I-5 after our coffee, and I started drivin'. And he says to me as I was goin' through the gears, 'Hey, Jack, you ever get one of these long-wheelbase trucks off the road?' And I said, 'Why gee, no, I haven't. How come you say that? Are they kind of squirrely?' And he said, 'Just keep it on the road,' and he went in the sleeper."

Marty has to leave for meet-and-greets. He introduces me to Jack first. Talk to this man, he says. For the next two hours, I am educated by way of parable and digression. Kindly and attentively, as though he were the one lucky to be there, Ramblin' Jack Elliott talked of thirteen-speed split shifts, good horses, the trim of a schooner, and the feel of a stiff guitar pick. He told me about "Muleskinner Blues," and later he joined Marty onstage and sang it. "What key do you do it in?" asked Marty, back on the bus, prior. "A or E, I can't remember," said Jack. "Don't worry, we'll find ya," says Marty. Then Jack says he called Guy Clark to say hello late last year, and Townes Van Zandt was on the phone. Townes is dead six months now, and at the mention of his name, the talk turns softer. The road manager checks in, asks about Jack sitting in for two songs. "We ain't fer sure of the key yet," says Jack. "Don't worry," says Marty. "You pick one. We'll blunder in behind ya. Always wanted to be in your band."

Anyway, country rocker Marty Stuart and old folkie Ramblin' Jack Elliott: You've heard of the six degrees of Kevin Bacon? With Ramblin' Jack, *two* degrees is rara avis.

Back on the phone to California. Still not getting to the point, but having a good time avoiding it. Jack reins in a story, tries to do the proper interview thing.

"Y' wanna talk about guitar chords? Or picks? Tricks? Cases? Airlines?" You see how it goes.

Jan, in the background. Saying something that ends with
". . . *new album!*"

"Album!" Jack snickers like a kid hiding from his mother
on his night to do dishes.

I take a shot. "Here's the trouble: My editor and your producer will at some point probably expect that we mention the
new album, huh?"

"What magazine is this for?"

"*No Depression* magazine."

"Oh, right, *No Depression* magazine . . . that's cute."

I press on, none too eloquently. "Which actually, before I
ask you about the album stuff, I think, that magazine is, y'-
know, it's a young audience, it's kinda alternative country is
what it is. How d'you . . ." Jack pulls in without signaling,
cuts me off with a whopping non sequitur.

"Yeah, I was surprised, because I always got depressed
when I was in Seattle, even when I was truckin'. Oh, I like the
boats, I love the water up there. I had a wonderful adventure
rowin' around in a rubber raft on Lake Union one day, and
got picked up by a kid in a lifeboat who was sailing with a
homemade sail rig, made out of a transparent piece of Vis-
queen plastic sheet, a two-by-four for a mast, and some clothes-
line for riggin', and he was steerin' with an oar, he didn't
even have a rudder, but it was a real old, tiny little ship's
lifeboat off of some ferryboat, and he lived with his parents on some forty-five-foot yawl that was moored over the

yacht anchorage at the opposite side of the bay—the upwind
end of this Lake Union, which is full of all kinds of interesting ships. There's a big four-masted lumber schooner that
lives there called the *Wawona*, there's the Center for Wooden
Boats. . . ."

Which reminds me. All that talk about the stooped-over
voice, the colds, the bad hip, I've made him sound old. But
when he really gets going, when he's trying to explain to you
how that racing schooner he boarded in Guam gathered up the
wind and simply *disdained* the water, he drops the cowhand
growl and just plain *enthuses*. And when he laughs—usually at
a respectful distance following his own observations—it's one
of those half-and-half laughs. Half humor, half wonderment at
it all. Like, can you *believe* this life?

I'll skip ahead. Tell you that Ramblin' Jack never did get
around to commenting on the album. About the time my tape
was running out, he announced that *Friends of Mine* producer
Roy Rogers had just tracked mud into the house. "Let me introduce you to someone," I heard, and then Rogers was on
the phone. I saw this for the opportunity it was and decided to
make hay.

We talked about how a man who has written fewer than
five songs in his life has become such a universal touchstone.
"He's the link," said Rogers. "He was really the last guy to hit
the road with Woody, and he had such strong connections in

Europe, where the Rod Stewarts and the Mick Jaggers saw him in English folk clubs and he turned them on to American roots music.

"He's not well known to the general populace, and they don't understand how he knows all these people, or why they know him, but that's the way things have gone in our cultural context. There's all this division into musical camps. People don't understand . . . Jimmie Rodgers was a *pop* artist in his day. I asked Howlin' Wolf once, 'Where'd you get that yodel?' 'I listened to Jimmie Rodgers on the radio comin' outta Nashville,' he said. Not to get too scholastic, but when we chose the songs for this album, we wanted them to be representative of Jack's whole context." The context is there, not only in the songs, and the singers, but in the sound of the album. Listen to Ramblin' Jack singing Townes Van Zandt's "Rex's Blues," and you hear Townes. Of course, listen to Townes, and you hear Jack. And while I may be trying too hard, when I heard Jack's high harmony behind Tom Waits on "Louise," my first thought was of Sara Carter. When he joins up with Jerry Jeff Walker on "Hard Travelin' " and "He Was a Friend of Mine," you're hearing music written by Woody Guthrie and Bob Dylan, but you're also hearing how Ramblin' Jack informed country's outlaw movement. His take on Joe Ely's "Me and Billy the Kid" plants him in the midst of the Austin scene. And so on, right through pop rock (for those of us introduced to Tim Hardin's "Reason to Believe" via Rod Stewart), Nashville, and Deadhead land.

"It's just him, covering a lot of different territory in American music," said Rogers. "But we didn't set out to make a nostalgic record. He's not a historical guy, he's right here now." And for the record, for all its musical cross-references, the album doesn't come off as a look back. Even "Bleeker Street Blues," a recent, rare Elliott composition, is set firmly in the present. The history is there, the whole Woody/Jack/Bob thing, but in the end, the song is about context. The here and now, how we got here, how it looks, and what we yet dare wish for.

Landlocked in dark Minneapolis, fitsing-and-startsing through the wet stoplights, Jack is telling the driver sea stories. He's tiny in the front seat, all hunched shoulders and hat. The salt-spray hiss of the tires plays beneath the narration.

". . . He went out the yardarm, on the foot-rope. The halyard parted. The yard crushed him. *By Way of Cape Horn,* that's the name of the book," he says. "You should read it. It's in the 917.8s."

He'll talk about trucks. He'll talk about ships. He'll talk about the Dewey Decimal System, for crying out loud. But Jack . . . what about the music? What'll I tell people?

"Tell 'em my teeth are fallin' out, I can barely walk, and they better hurry up if they wanna see me, 'cuz I may not be around much longer." He's chuckling.

"But if I make it through this year, I'm gonna get me that 1947 Peterbilt and put another Cummins 220 in it, it's got a five and four, a long wheelbase, I'm gonna put an old Airstream trailer on the back of it, and man, we won't have to get on no god-damn airports *any*-more!"

I giggle. It's right there on the tape, completely unprofessional. But it gives Jack time to circle back along the yarn and come up with an answer.

"Tell 'em I'm nineteen."

1998

Steve Earle:
Hard-Core Troubador

Before you read this piece you need to know some
things:

- Steve Earle has been married six times.

- Steve Earle has poor driving habits.

- Steve Earle took a break from the making of music
  through the mid-1990s in order that he might
  increase his consumption of regrettable sub-
  stances, live in real bad parts of town and break a
  few traffic laws. Then he had a nice rest in jail.

- Steve Earle is bigger than I and has more tattoos.

- Steve Earle wrote and recorded "My Old Friend the
  Blues" long before the Proclaimers were proclaiming.

- Steve Earle sings country music without the aid
  of a Stetson, a belt buckle or a cute little butt.

- Steve Earle is the real deal.

- I like Steve Earle. Of course I've never had to
  ride with him. Or marry him.

CADOTT, WISCONSIN, 1994. Country Fest. Notebook in hand, I stand in darkness as six lovely boys who missed the White Lion reunion tour casting call get thirty thousand drunken cheeseheads in a cow pasture to hoist their thirty-fifth beer of the day to the night sky and scream "God Blessed Texas!" It occurs to me that something is drastically wrong.

GENEVA, SWITZERLAND, APRIL 27, 1996. Country Jamboree at the Palexpo. I was warned, and it's true: Many Swiss country music fans show up dressed in period clothing, including toy pistols, sheriff's badges and even a headdress or two. As a Confederate general prices felt cowboy hats in the lobby, his petticoated daughter stumbles over his dangling sabre.

CANNOCK, ENGLAND, APRIL 30, 1996. Since I was here last, seven years have passed. The coal mines have shut down. The surrounding farmland has disappeared under a mitotic profusion of two-story brick duplexes; meadow and gorse have been subdivided by tarmac strips dubbed Meadow Way and Gorse Lane. The traffic circles are jammed with young professionals fleeing the decay of nearby Birmingham, but crime is hitching a ride. The town council responded by filling the old town center with tulips, bandstand gazebos and cobblestoned doses of "quaint." Still, the council is under pressure to do more: Surveillance cameras—"like the ones in

Birmingham"—are on order. And then, the bad news: While
hiding out over coffee and a buttered scone at George and
Bertie's Tea Room—one of Cannock's surviving links to the
past—I hear the waitress tell the cook about her plans for Friday night: American line-dancing lessons. Seems it's the rage
in England at the moment. And to think they're all worked up
about Mad Cow Disease.

The day I left England for Switzerland, my English friend
Tim rose early to take me to the train, leaving him no time to
make his usual two sandwiches. And so, at lunch, he went to a
greasy truck stop near his work site. A big ugly trucker was
just finishing his chips; Tim asked if he could have the
trucker's newspaper. The trucker grunted and pushed it
Tim's way. Somewhere in the middle-of-nowhere pages, a
tiny concert notice caught his eye. Steve Earle and the Dukes,
Birmingham Town Hall. Having endured my raves about an
Earle show I'd seen in March, he got on the phone immediately and secured a set of tickets.

I knew nothing of this as I walked home from George and
Bertie's, heavy laden with thoughts of how the Nashvirus, no
longer confined to U.S. cow pastures, has infected Boot-
Scootin' Brits and Swiss cowpokes. When Tim called, he
asked if I'd be interested in seeing a band called the Dukes,
with some guy named Steve Earle. The wry British sense of
humor, you understand. He picked me up at six, and we

headed for Birmingham, against the nocturnal flow of subdivision-bound escapees.

BIRMINGHAM, ENGLAND. The Town Hall looks more like the Parthenon than a town hall. Steve Earle lumbers on-stage and renders the point moot: within six bars of "Feel Alright," the joint's a roadhouse. Next, he rocks through "Hard-Core Troubador," and further stomps all over the notion that rehab and living in Nashville may have deadened his muse. Indeed, each of the eleven songs he performed from the twelve-song *I Feel Alright* album (the second since his infamous "vacation in the ghetto") stand as proof of his artistic survival. His penchant for diplomacy has survived, as well: Explaining why none of the *I Feel Alright* songs will be released as a single in England, he quips, "It's because . . . well, it's because we're sick of kissin' [BBC] Radio One's ass." Cheers all around. Curmudgeonry is replaced with a twinkling eye, however, when he grins over the opening chords of "My Old Friend the Blues," and says, "Here's an old Proclaimers song."

Midway through the show, the Dukes vacate the stage, leaving Earle to solo with an acoustic guitar and harmonica. As he did in Minneapolis, Earle performs "State Trooper," from Bruce Springsteen's *Nebraska*, introducing it as a song written by "a hillbilly from New Jersey." He introduces "Valentine's Day" with the humorous tale of how the song came about as a result of his being legally deprived of the right to drive. Earle's habit of bracketing lyric lines with audible breaths is powerfully emotive in an acoustic setting; during "Ellis Unit One," written for *Dead Man Walking*, the effect is positively chilling.

As the Dukes rejoin him, Earle tunes up for "Billy and Bonnie." "How y'all doin'?" he asks the crowd. A few "al-rights" are heard, but from my darkened back-row balcony seat, your humble reviewer inexplicably bellers, *"All the way from Wisconsin, man!"* Earle stops dead. "Wisconsin! Damn!" Next, I devolve completely from objective concert critic to blatant panty-tossing teenie-bopper fan mode: *"Woooooo!!!!"* Earle plays the opening riff, then stops again. "Wisconsin! I thought I was a long way from home. Man, you're lost!" By this time humiliation and the fear of being beat up by the main attraction has enabled me to shut up. The rest of the show is like blastin' down a back road in a badass hot rod; things just keep gettin' faster and louder. By the time we scream into "Guitar Town," the English have stormed the stage, and my buddy Tim has sung himself hoarse. I find myself desperately wishing all those Little Texas fans could be here. I want to fly in the Swiss family Confederate, get them vaccinated against the Nashvirus for life. I want that tea room waitress next to me pistoning her fist to "Copperhead Road," thoroughly purged of the need to ever again hook her thumbs in her belt loops.

But nothing's worse than a proselytizer; they gotta get it on their own. So until they do, lemme preach to the choir: The coal mines are gone, but Steve Earle is back. Lordy, is he back. Makes me wanna holler.

1996

☺ ☺ ☺

P.S. From the moment I heard "Guitar Town," Steve Earle had me revved up to run. I remember standing on the deck of a John Deere B, raking hay with the throttle wide open and *Exit 0* on the headphones, my heart impatient, the highway on my mind. His work has driven me deep into many a night. Whatever the state of his life or politics, his music has never once wasted my time, and indeed, has influenced my work on the level of my favorite poet, Dylan Thomas. Despite my hard-core fan status, in 2000 I wrote a review for *No Depression* magazine implying that *Transcendental Blues*, the album Earle released that year, probably wasn't going to do much for his career. It became his best-selling album ever.

Regarding the state of mainstream country music, it remains largely bad pop music, but I have learned to stop being so snooty on the subject.

IV. The Body Eclectic

Scarlet Ribbons

The man in the small room with me is a convicted murderer. He is immense and simple, looks as if he was raised on potatoes and homemade biscuits. I'd lay money that before he wound up here, his clothes smelled of bacon grease. He knows I am uneasy. I know he knows, because he looked me square in the eye, grinned, and told me so. Still, *The New York Times Magazine* has given me an assignment, and although I may be edgy in this prison, in this room with concrete blocks close all around, with this bulky killer two feet away, I must complete it.

I am to determine if the prisoner is happy.

The first person to whom I ever administered an intramuscular injection was a cheery wee granny. I see her still, seated on a hospital chair, flannel gown hiked up to expose her left quadriceps, head fluffed with a blessing of fine white curls, smile as sweet and warm as a batch of sugar cookies. The steel needle is cocked an inch from her skin, and she chirps: "Have you ever done this before?"

"Oh yes," I lie. Brightly. Smoothly. Never breaking eye contact.

Heraclitus said you can never step in the same river twice. Jorge Luis Borges said time is forever dividing itself toward innumerable futures—that we choose one alternative at the expense of all others. We can never be who we set out to be, but will always be who we were. I went to college to become a nurse. I became a writer. We spring from a thicket of tangents. I remember the exact moment I decided to become a nurse. I was reading *Sports Illustrated* in the high school library. I was supposed to be in World Literature, but the university recruiter was in town, and we were allowed to skip class to catch her pitch. I signed up, but once in the library, headed straight for the magazine rack, lolling through *People* and *Newsweek* while the rest of the students joined the recruiter at a long table. Late in her presentation, I overheard her reciting a list of majors: "Biology. Business. Economics. History. Nursing."

Nursing, I thought. *That sounds interesting.*

I filled out the necessary paperwork, and reported for class in the fall.

Nursing is so easily caricatured by white skirts and chilly bedpans. Pills and needles. Shots. But this is like saying painting is about paint. Practiced at its best, nursing is humane art, arisen from intimate observation and expressed through care. Again and again our instructors reminded us that every patient is a point of convergence, an intersection of body, mind, and spirit. We were trained to obtain quantifiable data with stethoscopes and sphygmomanometers, but we were also warned not to ignore intuition. We learned to change sheets without removing a bedridden patient, we learned how to prevent decubitus ulcers by monitoring pressure points, we learned to stick lubricated feeding tubes up noses, but we also learned to seek eye contact, perceive nonverbal communication, and establish trust so rapidly that within five minutes of meeting a stranger we could quite comfortably inquire after his bowel habits. Facilitate, reflect, and clarify; employ empathic response. These are the interviewing tools of the nurse. Also eminently functional, as it turns out, in the service of interviewing murderers for *The New York Times*. Every time I filled a syringe, I was filling my writer's pen with ink.

Heraclitus also said we are never being, but becoming, and in between clinical rotations and classes on skin disease, all nursing students were required to enroll in humanity courses. This rankled me. I have never been taken with the concept of a liberal arts education. The idea of lounging around dissecting *Tom Jones* when I should have been dissecting piglets always struck me as mark-time dawdling along the road to employability. I'd change out of surgical scrubs and hustle off to badminton class, Econ 110, or The United States Since 1877, or Introduction to Film, or Introduction to Creative Writing, or Folk Music in America. I expected the Chemistry 210, the General Zoology, the Developmental Psych and the Survey of Biochemistry, and willingly submitted to the Minnesota Multiphasic Personality Inventory assessment designed to reassure the beehived matron at the helm of the nursing school that I was unlikely to bite my patients or develop perverse affections for iodine swabs, but a .5 credit course in relaxation? What did these things have to do with nursing? Peering into the thicket of tangents, I saw nothing but obstruction.

Early one morning during a summer O.R. rotation, long before most people had finished their first cup of coffee, a surgeon inflated and deflated a lung for me. It pressed out of the patient's bisected chest like a greasy trick balloon, then shrunk back and retreated into a cheesy lump beside the patient's writhing heart. The mechanics were fascinating. Here was the corporeal gristle revealed. We tote our organs around not even knowing them. There is nothing abstract about a glistening length of intestine. But by drawing back the curtain, the surgeon managed to reframe the mystery. Now that I had peeked behind the liver, eyed the discrete lumps of organ, I wondered where the spirit might lie. It's one thing to speak of the heart as a center of emotion, quite another to see it lurching between the lungs like a spasmodic gray slug. We were as deep in the body as you can get—exactly where did they keep the soul? The finite, meaty nature of it all blunted my ability to imagine the body as a place for spirits.

When I was a child, my father, a quietly eccentric farmer, would sometimes come in the house after the evening milking, rustle up his blighted trumpet and play "A Trumpeter's Lullaby." We sat at his feet, and he swayed above us, an overalled gnome, eyes closed, gently triple-tonguing the wistful passages. The notes twined from the brass bell in liquescent amber, settling over our hearts and shoulders, wreathing us in warm, golden light. Many years later I found myself standing at a meds cart in a surgical ward, sorting pills into cups, chafing in my polyester student nurse smock, short of sleep and overwhelmed by my patient care assignments, desperately trying to sort out the drug interactions before my instructor arrived to grill me on the same, when "A Trumpeter's Lullaby" came seeping from the speaker in the ceiling. I was swept with a desperate melancholy. I have never been so lonely. And try as I might, I could not see how the path on which I stood could be backtracked to the feet of my trumpeting father. In more dramatic circumstances, I might have stripped off my smock, gobbled the meds and run off to join an agrarian brass band, but my instructor appeared and began to ask me if there was any danger in administering diazepam and clonidine in tandem. I fidgeted, answered hopefully and resumed forward motion.

After four years, I took my nursing boards, convinced I'd fail, and passed just fine. Worked as a nurse for a while and liked it. But I kept having trouble remembering all the numbers, and how Demerol interacted with Elavil, and just what it was phagocytes did, and yet I could remember the poem the stunted guy behind me in creative writing wrote about electrical high lines, and what the professor said it lacked, and how I believed the high line guy could have done better, and how I remembered the way the folk music professor crossed his legs and fingered his guitar when he explained that the scarlet ribbons in "Scarlet Ribbons" weren't ribbons at all, but bright blood on a child's fractured head, and I thought of the lung puffing and falling, and I said if I can conjure these things so easily while I stumble over drug interactions and hematocrits, perhaps I ought to write instead. I took to talking about this. Overfrequently, apparently, because one day my girlfriend said, "Why don't you stop talking about it and do it?"

And so I did.

There was much to learn, but much less to unlearn.

. . .

I wonder if Heraclitus would dare tell the prisoner he was not stepping in the same river twice. A lifetime of days between those tan concrete blocks? Sounds like the same old river to me. Still, our little visit must have been a diversion. I imagine he chuckled with his roomie later when he described catching me in my unease. It was a fair cop. But as he leaned in and grinned, I slid the needle in and drew out what I needed. When I stepped out of the prison, it was cold and windy, but the waning light seemed to propose an answer.

2000

Rock Slide!

When *Men's Health* ran this piece about my first-ever kidney stone, they decorated it with a John Manno photograph of a big jagged rock jammed in a cheap plastic funnel. Exactly.

○ ○ ○

In the end, what I remember most is how I would find myself *peeing hopefully*. I'd stand there over the bowl, with my little strainer in one hand and me in the other, and I'd be thinking, *This time . . . maybe this time*. And then I would finish, shake loose the last little drop, and *nothing*. Over and over again, five, six . . . ten times a day, for eleven days, from February into March, I'd peer into that strainer with the cheated pout of a little boy who finishes his Cracker Jacks and finds no prize.

I had a kidney stone in me, and I wanted it out.

The stone struck on a Tuesday evening, somewhere along I-94 just east of Minneapolis. First came an upper-abdominal twinge, similar to gas pains at dawn (of the sort precipitated— I'm from Wisconsin—by excess bratwurst at bedtime), except that no amount of twisting or turning would break it loose. Then it seemed as if my right kidney had been run through with a superheated knitting needle. I was veering in and out of my lane, gasping like a scuppered carp. Struck by this delusion that a hot bath would dissipate the pain, I careened to a motel. I'm certain the desk clerk pegged me for a meth fiend—I was pallid, shivering, and rolling in sweat as she ran my credit card— but she worked quickly. I staggered to the room, filled the tub full blast and stripped out of my clothes.

By now, based on my experience as a nurse and an EMT, I had pretty much self-diagnosed. One in ten Americans will experience the joy of kidney stones, and the pain I felt was my secret handshake into the club. I dropped into the steaming water and—drawing on my knowledge of anatomy, physics, and desperation—assumed a bizarre position calculated to roll the stone back into the kidney. (When Ben Franklin's kidney stone blocked his bladder, he used to stand on his head to pee.) After about fifteen seconds of lying in scalding water with my butt hoisted above the Plimsoll mark, I ran up the white flag and dialed 911.

On a pain scale of 1 to 10, kidney stones consistently ring the bell at 10. A mother of three who had a kidney stone once told me, "I'd rather give birth three times—in one day!" The pain is focused, relentless, and inescapable. I pride myself on a certain blue-collar hardiness and Scandinavian stoicism, but by the time a paramedic arrived, I was flailing around the motel room bed spewing effenheimers. "Bet it's a kidney stone," said the paramedic. "Morphine?"

"Oh, yeah," I hissed.

While he slid the needle in, I puked into a bag. Puking is a classic kidney-stone symptom, caused by overstimulation of stomach nerves. The morphine helped, but I was still twisting like a bug pinned to a board when they strapped me to the cot. In Woodbury, Minnesota, a nurse in the Woodwinds Health Campus E.R. gave me another bump of morphine, but during a CT scan the pain came stabbing back. The nurse pushed a drug called Toradol. Sweet relief. I dozed until the E.R. doc woke me. "It's fairly large, as stones go," he said. "It's borderline whether it will pass on its own." The next time I woke, my father and brother had arrived to retrieve me and my car. The nurse handed me a bottle of Percocet and a screened funnel. "Strain your urine," she said, "and save the stone." I tottered out the door, paused to puke in the parking lot, and set out for home.

I spent the week at my parents' farmhouse in Wisconsin. Now and then the pain would outdistance the Percocet, and I would try anything—hot baths, microwaved hot packs, incessant pacing—to distract myself until the drugs caught up. Once I was crawling out of the bathtub when I was swept with nausea. I scrambled for the toilet. Hearing the scuffle, my mom burst in to check on me, and so it was that at the age of thirty-seven I found myself buck naked on all fours, head in the toilet, puking at the feet of dear old Mom. She's been a nurse for forty years and was unfazed, but a guy hopes for a little dignity.

The Percocet beat most of the pain and gave me freaky dreams. But it also made me more pukey, and since I couldn't keep anything down, I began to fall behind on my fluid intake. Not good when you're relying on hydraulic forces to flush a stone. On day three, the knitting needle woke me with a vengeance. Back to the E.R. "You got Toradol?" I asked. They did. By this time I was peeing thimblefuls of what appeared to be scorched corn syrup. They kept me overnight, pumped me full of fluids and sent me home with Compazine to treat the nausea. Because long-term use of Toradol can affect kidney function, the doctor was reluctant to prescribe the pills, but I promised to use them only during peak pain moments. One kidney stone, three days, and I had become a craven junkie.

And so I pounded fluids and waited. I'd go an entire day without pain, then zing, it would be back. The stone was moving through the ureter toward the bladder. It was almost even with my hip bone. I took my little strainer everywhere. I carried it in my coat pocket, wrapped in a plastic bag. In public restrooms, I'd go into the stall (you really can't stand at a urinal in the Farm & Fleet peeing through a funnel and expect to escape arrest or injury), and I'm sure when people heard the crackle of the plastic they thought, *Drugs! Perversion!* Then there was the problem of rinsing the thing off. I resorted to feet checks and strategically timed dashes. Kidney stones are all about drugs and furtiveness.

Researchers have identified nineteen distinct types of kidney stones.

"Twenty, actually!" says Michael Rentzepis, M.D. He is a urologist in private practice. Nine days since the first attack and still no stone, so I was referred to him for a consultation. Dr. Rentzepis is young and trim. He has the large glasses and eager demeanor of your classic science geek, which I find to be a comfort, doctorwise. "A new variation has just been discovered!" he says. Excitement has drawn him right to the edge of his chair.

"Well, now," I say. "That'll be the talk of the annual urology convention."

"Oh, yes," says Dr. Rentzepis. He's lit up like a grade-schooler describing the new teeter-totter. "It's just like adding another element to the periodic table!"

Bless his heart, my urologist is a geek for renal calculi.

"Let's look at your CT scan," says Dr. Rentzepis.

I was once arc welding the underside of an equipment

trailer when a molten pearl of slag dripped into my welding gauntlet, lodging against my fingernail. The pain was astounding. Flinging everything, I yipped and scooted from beneath the trailer like a poodle suffering a buttful of rock salt. On the CT scan, the kidney stone is an incandescent dot amid all the halftone grays. I think immediately of the molten slag droplet, sliding lazily through my ureter, burning white-hot until it finally plops into the watery bladder and the pain stops.

"The stone is right at the end of the ureter," says Dr. Rentzepis, pointing at the bright dot. "Almost out. Trouble is, a stone of this size, it's about fifty-fifty whether or not it'll pass on its own."

"What are my options?"

"Generally," says Dr. Rentzepis, "you want to let it pass. Although removal procedures are straightforward, you can have complications." He pulls out a comic book: *Understanding Kidney Stones*. On the cover, a golfer clutches his back, his sweaty face gripped in a rictus of pain. On page ten, a man is reclining in a tub while shock waves blast his stone to bits. Lithotripsy. Relatively painless, but the truck-mounted portable unit isn't due in town this week. On page twelve, a doctor inserts a tube in the patient's back, blasts the stone with ultrasound, and plucks out the fragments, a treatment reserved for stones over one inch in diameter. My stone is big, but not that big. Another series of illustrations demonstrates how staghorn stones—huge things with spikes and projections—require surgical removal and a four-day hospital stay. "I'll put a ureteroscope in your urethra, through your bladder, and up to the stone," says Dr. Rentzepis. "I'll pluck the stone with a little caliper-like device." No incisions. But right up the old main line. "Then we'll probably need to put a tube in the ureter for a few days, to keep it from swelling shut."

"Do you have to go back up there to get the tube out?"

"Oh, no," says Dr. Rentzepis. "We tie a string to it. After a few days, you come into the office and I'll pull it out."

"Umm . . . let's give it another couple days."

I was caught completely off guard when it finally happened. I was visiting friends. We were leaving to see a band, and I had run upstairs for a quick filtered pee. Urinating through a sifter was second nature by now, and my mind was somewhere else when—*boooiing!*—there was a sudden rubbery back pressure, my urine flow stopped dead, my bladder expanded, then, *Clack!* and I was peeing effortlessly again. You know how sometimes if you turn the faucet off too quickly the pipes rattle? There's a term for that. It's called water hammer. When that kidney stone hit the homestretch, I had my own little water-hammer moment. And now there it was: dark brown, rock-hard, and the size of a chokecherry pit. I had a sudden urge to call friends and hand out cigars. Instead I rinsed the stone and looked at it closely. It was studded with tiny nubs and felt like sandpaper. I got a little creeped out and light-headed then.

I went to my follow-up appointment. No sooner had he closed the examining room door than Dr. Rentzepis turned to me eagerly. "Did you bring it?" It was like in third grade when Vinnie Boscoe wondered if you'd brought the fart cushion. I pulled the specimen bottle from my pocket and held it up to view. The stone rattled against the plastic. Dr. Rentzepis's eyes widened.

"Oh my God!"

Can I tell you what pride it gives a man to produce a thing in this way and have a board-certified urologist say, "Oh my God!"? I averted my eyes, flushed with aw-shucks pride. Just as quickly, I drew back.

"I bet you tell all your patients that."

"Oh, no," he said. "That really is a big one. Stones of that size, we usually have to go in after them."

I was glowing.

Dr. Rentzepis has known patients to mount their stones in resin. He made me turn mine in. He sent it to a lab to be crushed and analyzed. It was 80 percent calcium oxalate and 20 percent calcium phosphate. The most common sort. Based on that information, he says I have to drink twelve glasses of water a day for the rest of my life, basically to keep my system flushed, as recurrence rates run about 80 percent.

("Once a stone thrower, always a stone thrower," said my regular M.D. when he visited me in the E.R.) I'll also drop in for an abdominal Xray now and then, in the hope that we'll catch the next one earlier. Before we hit the "Oh my God" stage.

The French essayist Montaigne wrote that kidney stones left him feeling great intellectual clarity. No sign of that so far. But I have noticed changes. I try to drink more water. Where I used to tolerate tales of childbirth with a sort of deferential politeness, I now find myself nodding in solidarity. And when I looked across the median of I-80 during a recent road trip and saw a westbound semi emblazoned with the words *American Kidney Stone Management*, I got so misty I nearly left the roadway. Somewhere out there someone else was gasping like a scuppered carp, and here, apparently piloted by angels, was a white Kenworth, its hood ornament aimed at kidney stones everywhere. Sweet, sweet relief, *hammer down*.

2002

Life in the Fat Lane

I knew writing an article like this without upsetting someone would be a tricky proposition. Several months after it hit print, I was at a family reunion. One of my aunts, whose metabolism is stacked against her, approached me. "I saw your 'fat' article when I was checking out at the grocery store," she said. "I had to buy the magazine to see just what you had to say." I looked at her like a cornered dog who spots someone approaching with a rolled-up newspaper. "I think you did all right." She smiled. "It didn't seem like you were picking on anyone." I began to breathe again. Never mind literary critics in ivory towers. It's aunts at reunions who can cut your career short.

○   ○   ○

You look like you've put on some weight. Think I'm rude? Insensitive? Sorry, but the experts and their numbers back me up. Diane Dresel is the Coordinator of Health Management Resources at Midelfort Clinic in Eau Claire, Wisconsin: "We have an epidemic of obesity going on," she says. Obesity is defined as weighing 20 percent more than your ideal body weight, and things are especially heavy in Wisconsin. "We are trend leaders in obesity," says Dresel. "Although, I think we did drop to number two in the nation last year." To make matters worse, during winter in Wisconsin, most of us eat more and move less. Extra weight tends to stack up like snow in a supermarket parking lot, with one significant difference: Come springtime, the snow melts. Not so the accumulations of adiposity.

Of course, it isn't just the obese who fight the wintertime bulge. Ever since I got within a fork's length of thirty, I've had an on-again, off-again relationship with an extra ten pounds. I don't obsess about it, but I do check the bathroom scale out of the corner of my eye now and again. I have been blessed with a metabolism that up to this point, at least, can be harassed into service, commandeered into burning away the winter's belt-line buildup. But when it comes to people who eat too much, I have empathy—which, as any therapist worth their weight in diplomas will assure you, is more important than sympathy. Because I love to eat. Oh, I eat my vegetables, and fiber is my friend. But nobody is a bigger fan of the empty calorie than yours truly. If it comes packaged in crinkly plastic, I'll eat it. If the sugar content hovers in the range of "pure cane octane," give me two. If artificial flavor is involved, so am I. And chocolate? Forget it. I've eaten enough chocolate in the past two years to double dip the Bloomer water tower like a big ol' marshmallow Easter egg.

And so, I have been approached by the editors of this magazine to address the problem in print. I'm sure they trust I will lend some sort of insight, tap some hidden source of knowledge, come up with nifty pun-intensive sidebars the likes of "Ten Surefire Weighs (wink) to Drop Pounds Without Lifting a Finger."

I wish. I'd be on a national book tour so fast it would make your bathroom scale spin.

Oh, it's not as though you don't have options. Wisconsin may lead the way to the buffet, but the obsession with thinness is a national one and it has spawned an industry eager to slim you down. Trouble is, no matter how honest they may be, somewhere along the line they all tend to have a ring of the snake oil salesman about them. According to one brochure, from a national weight loss organization, ". . . most diets allow just limited foods, and they don't teach you how to stay in control once you've lost weight." Of course, this begs the question: Do they offer a diet that allows unlimited foods? Read on, and it sure sounds like it: "Our Fat & Fiber plan offers remarkable flexibility for those of you who need the freedom to eat just about anything, anywhere." Really. Well, make mine funnel cakes at the fair. More from the brochure:

". . . eat the foods you love while you follow our plan."
Hmm. The foods I love—does your plan include chocolate-covered cherries and cheddarwurst?

When they're not making statements that stretch credulity, weight loss organizations often lapse into a fog of euphemisms. I've memorized a few, and intend to use them the next time I order breakfast at the local café: "And a lovely good morning to you, Cecille. Listen, as of this morning I am on a quest to make better food choices through problem solving and goal setting. I am seeking net physique enhancement.

"That being so, I am concerned with portion control and wish to avoid calorically dense foodstuffs, as well as significant fat sources. So whaddya got?" After a moment of silence, during which you could hear a fat-free corn curl drop, Cecille will probably shove a plateful of cheezy hash browns my way and say, "Here. Eat this. You'll feel better." And you know what? I will. And that's the problem. We love this stuff. It does make us feel better. That's what the dieters, dieticians, the diet centers, the weight counselors, the unsalted Styrofoam chips, are up against. We know we should eat more fresh vegetables and less fat. But when's the last time you turned on the football game, kicked back the recliner, popped the top on a mineral water and proceeded to gorge yourself on celery sticks? Can you imagine tailgate parties at Lambeau Field featuring fiber? People arriving three hours before the game to fill galvanized stock tanks with ice water and mixed veggies? Stuffing down rice cakes and apple slices? I didn't think so.

Of course not everyone requires a national organization to lose weight. Americans are notorious for their do-it-yourself diets. All this self-starting can lead to trouble, however. "People tend to go on these crash diets," says Dresel. "They fast for a week. That's not going to work. You need to change your lifestyle." To make matters worse, dieters often gain more weight back than they originally lost—weight loss literature refers to this as the "yo-yo effect." And then there's this passage, a warning from another national weight reduction organization to amateur dieters everywhere: "Most dieters who achieve significant weight loss lose far too much lean body mass (muscle and organ tissue). This not only diminishes strength and agility but also affects appearance. With less muscle, pleasing curves flatten, chests sink, arms and legs look spindly." That does it. Pass the chicken-fried steak.

None of this is helped by the Wisconsin winter. Not only does the miserably cold weather make us want to eat, it makes us want to hibernate. Activity levels drop with the mercury.

So why fight it? Is thin all it's cracked up to be? You have to believe that the members of the National Association to Advance Fat Acceptance (NAAFA) were heartened by the recent Kate Moss controversy. You remember Kate Moss. She's the supermodel who looks like she just gave blood—all of it.

Eyes like two vacant lots. A belly you could use to scoop bird seed. Kate caused a bit of controversy when a handful of social commentators commentated that her popularity places unrealistic pressure on American women to seek acceptance through thinness. Diane Dresel is all for thinness, but within reason. "We're not talking about making Twiggys [Twiggy was Kate Moss, circa the '60s] out of everybody. We're talking about a healthy lifestyle. Size acceptance is important. You need to accept people at any weight, like any height. Persons with weight problems are treated like second-class citizens. As a clinician, I'd like to see greater understanding of obesity. It's a chronic disease of lifestyle, the same as alcoholism. It has a high rate of relapse. If the alcoholic relapses and goes back to treatment, we say, 'good for you.' With weight, we tend to say the person has no self-control or willpower. That's not the issue. We tell people you can like yourself but you don't have to like the weight." Perhaps some of this thinking is gaining a foothold: Lately, Kate Moss has been elbowed off the runway by wide-shouldered women with actual hips—not just hip bones. (It is interesting to note the part the weight loss industry plays in the Twiggy/Kate drama: Of fifteen people pictured in the brochure of one national organization, fourteen were women. The implicit message appears to be that it is less socially acceptable for a woman to be overweight than a man.)

So. You don't want the waif look, but you would like to

fend off the ten pounds brought to you by Wisconsin delicacies and Wisconsin winter. What's the answer? Well, I've done all the research for you. I called experts, I read brochures, I looked in my refrigerator. Heck, I burned enough calories punching my way around the endless loop of the automated Weight Watchers phone-mail system alone to earn myself a banana split (with a big white dose of that whipped cream in a can—a marvel of modern culinary engineering). But after all that work, I'm afraid what I have to say is less than thrilling. Whether you do it yourself or with the help of professionals, winter weight maintenance boils down to five words: *Eat less and move more.*

There you are. Plain and simple. Surely after all that talk about empty calories, you didn't think I'd sugarcoat it. 'Course, if I could get my hands on some chocolate . . .

1996

○ ○ ○

P.S. I saw my aunt yesterday. She was serving up a nice bowl of three-bean salad. I haven't seen Kate Moss for years. And this just in: EAT LESS. EXERCISE MORE.—front page, *USA Today*, July 19, 2004

Manure Is Elemental

In what I have come to count as my ear-
liest memory (these things are never certain), I
am backing away from a dog. It is a short-
haired dog, a herding dog, and it has backed
me down the dark end of a barn. The dog is
likely just curious, but her eyes are steadfast,
and she advances with her nose extended
stiffly. There is no sound but the flat-footed
scrape of my heels as I edge them behind me
like curb feelers. Far away up the concrete
walk, the barn door is an open rectangle of
light, but the dog is yielding nothing.

I am a farm boy, but this is not my barn. It
belongs to a farmer from our congregation. It is
a summer Sunday, and his wife has invited us to
dinner. Church is over, but I remain dressed
like a little Mister: trousers, dress shoes, a

clean button shirt. The dog moves in, chesty and intent. I edge back again, and this time there is nothing beneath my heels. I tumble backward into the gutter. The dog spooks at the sudden movement, dipping her haunches and flaring to one side, but shortly her nose is poking along the gutter edge above me. I can see whitewashed rafters.

The manure is mud-bath soft and blackstrap dark. Above all, it smells sweet. It is not so deep that I am in any danger, but I am well over three-quarters marinated. I don't remember any panic or fear, perhaps because I had broken the spell of the dog, but I must have called out, because my father appeared and pulled me from the muck. I was soon stripped of my togs and shivering under the garden hose. I assume the smell tarried well into the week.

It is a persistent scent. Years later in high school, I demonstrated a commitment to personal grooming so avid my peers saw fit to vote me Biggest Primper, Class of 1983. Despite my dedication, I found it impossible to cut the cow scent below levels detectable out of context. Beneath the English Leather the sweet note of dung did linger. I was one of those well-scrubbed small-town boys who sat beside you at the basketball game, and upon removing a coat donned in a porch hung with chore clothes, released a layer of trapped air that rose warmly to your nose, and you thought, *farm kid.*

When you are raised on a dairy, manure is elemental. Lactation cycles wax and wane, but cows produce manure full-time. Once a day we ran the barn cleaner, a motorized device that drew heavy iron paddles along the gutter bottom. The cows stood with their rears to the gutter but tended to undershoot. We used a wooden-handled scraper to clean up the misses. In winter, the firm, high-fiber pats scraped neatly, like ginger cookies off a baking tin. In spring, when the cows were on fresh grass and clover, the experience was more analogous to troweling prune smoothies.

Sometimes, if viscosity allowed, my brother and I went manure surfing. We adopted a hang-ten stance, standing sideways in the channel, booted goofballs being towed around the barn on a mile-an-hour hillbilly thrill ride, jumping off just before the manure passed through a hole in the wall and up an elevated chute. At the apex of the chute, the paddles swung into open air, leaving the clods and straw to fall into the manure spreader parked below.

I often volunteered to spread the manure, as this meant I could drive the tractor through the fields rather than stay behind to sweep the walk and shake out fresh straw. The manure spreader was a simple and spectacular machine. I'd gauge the wind (spread manure *with* the wind and you will come home speckled), engage the power takeoff, hit the throttle and let 'er rip. The beaters flung the manure in a skyward arc. What you had was a portable sludge fountain. In the winter, I'd look back and see the wide brown stripe and feel like I was finger painting a forty-acre canvas. December through February, we never stowed the spreader in the shed until it had been scraped down fore and aft, the beaters flossed like so many snaggled teeth. Too much residual manure would freeze up around the mechanisms, and the next time you engaged the power something snapped—a shear pin, a worm gear, the apron chain.

I can't say I miss the manure. I spent enough time on the wooden end of a pitchfork to view it primarily as something to be shoveled. Years of kneeling down to milk cows only to get smacked across the face with an excrement-drenched tail plume tempered my affection for the medium. As did having the bad luck to pass behind a cow just as she sneezed. The effect is jaw-dropping, although that would not be your optimal response.

I have a buddy who has watched his farm become a suburb. He gets hassled now when he runs his spreader. People object to the smell. Things change. I am not going to get elegiac. But I'm glad cow manure is one of the trace elements of my existence. It inoculated me against everything to follow. Gave me an organic sense of calibration. Wherever I am, whatever I face, I think of me looking up and that dog looking down. What a delightful place to start. As children, my siblings and I crossed the pasture using cow pies as stepping-stones. We pressed through the crust with our bare feet and relished in the squish. Certain self-regarding health spas in New Mexico will charge you one house payment for equivalent pleasures.

2004

Hirsute Pursuits

Despite what this piece says, I'm not twenty-eight anymore. I'm also still a ways from bald. But things ain't gettin' any thicker.

○ ○ ○

Over ten years ago, while clambering over an oil drilling rig, I fell headlong down a flight of twenty-five steel steps and knocked myself unconscious. While I sustained no long-term damage, the event was marked by a small scar just inside my hairline.

Recently, while peering in the mirror, I made a relevatory discovery: For future retellings of the "I-fell-off-an-oil-rig" story, it is no longer necessary that I part my hair to reveal the scar that verifies the tale.

Yep, at the relatively tender age of twenty-eight, it has become clear that I am losing the hair war. For nearly a quarter of a century, my scalp was protected by rank legions of hair. Then came the thinning of the ranks—followed by a general retreat from the front. These days, I don't so much comb my hair as harvest it—can complete surrender be far behind?

Bald. The word itself drops flat and ugly from the tongue. It has no bounce, no redeeming phonic personality. Worse yet, it is employed in the description of items past their useful life; e.g., tires and old carpet. A simple lie becomes an outrageous prevarication when characterized as "bald-faced." Even its association with the regal fowl symbolic of our great nation has failed to lend any dignity to this monosyllabic utterance.

Ahh, but never has there been a better time to go bald . . . after all, this is the age of the infomercial, and for my money, nothing is more amusing than watching a rollicking half hour of hair replacement therapy (which usually features a celebrity whose hairline and career are both in a state of recess). Just try to beat the entertainment value of watching a rather delicate gentleman "thickening" hair with sprinkles of colored powder from what appears to be a pepper shaker. Lots of on-cue oohing and aahing occurs, and each sprinkle is accompanied by a series of dainty "pats" on the head. As entertaining as this is, it's not for me. I'd probably show up at parties looking as if I were afflicted with brown dandruff. Furthermore, I don't fancy spending a lot of time patting myself.

In another infomercial, a fast-talking gent spray paints bald spots, racing gleefully from pate to pate, insisting all the while that he's not spray painting. Again, a lot of patting is involved, and despite strategically lit "before and after" pictures, a little voice inside my head continues to suggest that the emperor has no hair.

Then there's the one where an earnest trio of folks in expensive clothing offer to relocate chunks of the hair you have *left* into the places your hair left *from*. Seems a little too much like gardening to me. Yet another company actually weaves faux hair into place. Weaving: Isn't that how they make rugs?

A major pharmaceutical company offers a hair-sprouting ointment that actually works, with two qualifications: Don't expect hair like Fabio; do expect a monthly pharmacy bill the size of Fabio's pecs.

And so, short of getting sprinkled, sprayed, plugged, woven, or refinanced, what is a balding man to do?

Support groups are available, but who wants to sit around moaning about hair loss with a bunch of bald guys? If I need someone to hold my hand while I go bald, what will happen when I start to get liver spots, or develop an arthritic thumb? No thanks. I shall call upon my reserves of Scandinavian stoicism and tough this one out on my own.

I suppose I could start wearing hats. I have noticed that a certain famous country music star (who is able, with a simple twist of the hips, to reduce groups of normally well-behaved women to screaming throngs of lingerie-tossing fanatics) is more likely to whistle a medley of Barry Manilow jingles than remove his Stetson in public. Methinks he is keeping something (or nothing) under his hat.

But I'm not really a hat guy. Oh, they're nice—and if I thought by wearing one I could reduce groups of normally well-behaved women to screaming throngs of lingerie-tossing fanatics, I might give it a shot—but I've never really gotten used to them. For one thing, when I played football, I had the biggest helmet on the team. When we were measured for our high school graduation caps, yours truly topped the circumference list. Same story in college. So finding headgear that fits comfortably is a challenge. Adjustable caps offer an option, but most of these are emblazoned with team logos or mildly profane aphorisms . . . not my style.

And so, as my forehead continues to expand (leaving me to savor the scintillating humor inherent in statements the likes of "Say there, Mac, yer forehead's turnin' into a five-head, yuk, yuk"), I think I'll just get on with life. After all, it's not as if something really critical were falling out—like my pancreas, for instance.

As in nearly all things, if you look hard enough, there is a bright spot to be found amidst all this hair loss. Unfortunately, it happens to be the reflection of my bathroom light.

1995

☺ ☺ ☺

P.S. Ten years later, I can tell you a man never forgets his first sunburned scalp.

Catching at the
Hems of Ghosts

It all ends in death, thank goodness for
that. The hurly-burly winds down slowly or ends
abruptly as a bug on a bumper, and we leave it to
the living to mark our departure. Generally, they
will arrange a funeral. I use the term loosely, and
inclusively. Any sort of celebration will do.

My sister died when she was five. I remember the funeral home gathering seemed a crush,
and I remember resenting that my family—
stoics, all of us—had to weep with all those
people watching, but then out in the sunny
country cemetery, the hot breeze smelling of
soil, my brother and I handling the tiny casket,
the weeping came in a cleansing rush, and this
time, it felt very near to joy. A high school
classmate put his arm around my shoulders, a
gracious gesture for a teenage boy, and I smiled

my thanks, but he couldn't know my tears had gone from bitter to sweet. At that moment, mourning was comfort enough.

We humans have long held that someone's kicking the bucket deserves commemoration. We dance, we wail, we shoot their ashes from a shotgun. Whatever our funerary customs—be they acoustic or baroque—we are grappling to draw conclusions from the dead on behalf of the living.

As a celebration, a funeral isn't necessarily a party. Tears are not confetti. But could there be a more glorious celebration than the tear-soaked funeral of Miller McDermott? Miller lived up the street from me. He was a short, bald man with eleven children. He installed furnaces, and I never heard him speak a word. Such was his reticence that his legion grandchildren and great-grandchildren called him Grandpa Shy. The local Catholic church was wall-to-wall with his neighbors and descendants, and choked-up children came to the front of the church to tell Grandpa Shy stories. A picture emerged of a man who quietly found a way to make half the people in this church feel like his favorite. Looking on from the backmost pew, I was swept by the thought of this unassuming man as the nexus of so much love, and I cried a little. I felt self-conscious later, afraid someone might think I was appropriating the family's grief for a man I hardly knew. But I was not bereaved. I was simply grateful to witness the legacy of this man. Tears seemed the only worthy offering. One by one, Grandpa Shy loved his broad family. Then he died, and they all loved him at once. Is there a finer reason for a funeral?

It took a funeral for me to see my father without the usual filial opacities. He was a city-bred factory refugee when he bought our little farm. A Czech neighbor gave him his first milk cow, told him when to plant his corn, and helped with the haying. The Czech was still milking cows and going strong at seventy when a Holstein kicked him in the head, triggering a bleed that killed him in short order. By the time we buried him, he and my dad had a twenty-five-year history of more days spent together than apart. The preacher had finished up graveside and I was walking back to my car when I stepped around a shrub and discovered my father standing apart and alone, his face tight with grief, his eyes stark. For the first time in my life, I saw him simply as a man missing his friend. I have been better with him ever since.

Funerals can be punishing and bleak. But they are also an opportunity to reset the bar, to rub cold shoulders with mortality. To look in the mirror and see ourselves gone. We view the body at the front of the room and wonder if the fled soul knows The Secret. Even a fuddled agnostic like me associates death with transcendence. Transcendence is forgiveness with wings. And so we sit in the pew, and we mourn, but we also long and hope. We are catching at the hems of ghosts.

My father's farm adjoined land owned by two Norwegian bachelor brothers named Art and Clarence. My brother Jud and I used to like to help them with the haying because their hay baler made smaller bales than ours, which made us feel stronger and taller. After we unloaded the wagons, we were

served weak lemonade from a blue mason jar. Art always referred to my brothers Jed, Jud and John as "Yed, Yud and Yon."

Art died while I was in high school. By the time Clarence
died, I had been away from home for a decade. I lived in the
city, near my grandmother, and so I drove her to the funeral.
It was a bitter January day. The tiny Lutheran church was
packed with neighbors I hadn't seen for years. Many were
farmers in awkward shoes, their hands thick, their shoulders
rounded by the closeness of the room. Here and there a tear
tracked down a ruddy cheek.

There was a fair contingent of little old ladies, some of
them conversing in stage whispers, and I was reminded of the
two elderly sisters who were notorious for crashing local funerals, clucking mournfully throughout, then scoring some eats.
You could do worse—funerals here can be described as buffet
with a body. The organist played, the soloist sang a gentle version of "In the Garden," and then we all joined in on Hymn
495, as posted. Your average Wisconsin Lutheran can turn
"Sweet Georgia Brown" into a funeral dirge, so the appropriate
mournful tones were achieved without great difficulty, although
we did tend to thin out and break down a little when we hit the
high parts; but like an old farm truck wheezing over a hill, we'd
pick up speed and volume on the downslope.

After the service, we reconvened in the church basement.
We sat elbow-to-elbow at folding tables, eating from paper
plates. There were brownies and bars, carrot cake with cream

cheese frosting, scotcharoos, and green Jell-O dessert. Open-face Cheez Whiz sandwiches dotted with sliced green olives or tiled with potato chips. Kool-Aid and coffee, both served in foam cups. I sat by Jimmy Volsruud. Our fathers used to put up hay together, and Jimmy and I helped, but once he invited me to his tree house to share his raisin stash.

It was good to see Jimmy after all the years had passed. I told him I had been leery of his raisins because I saw a daddy longlegs crawl out of the red Sun-Maid box. I long coveted Jimmy's bike, a hand-painted blue single-speed fitted with sissy bars and an orange banana seat. He seemed pleased to recall the bike, and we talked about popping wheelies.

Many of the people around us were of a generation that still knew how to "visit," and the basement was lively with conversation. There was a feeling in the room that time had been condensed, that we were being allowed a quick trip back, celebrating the end of Clarence's years by reconvening them. Jimmy and I, with little in common now, were smiling over shared days, the divergent arcs of our lives meeting one more time at the point where Clarence's life ended. Sometimes we rail at death's thievery. Sometimes we cherish what death leaves behind.

Grandma was ready to go. I pulled the car around to the church steps, and got the door. As we pulled away, I said what we often say in these circumstances, "It was a good funeral."

"Yes," agreed Grandma. "Everyone had a real nice time."

2001

V. Way Off Main Street

What We Want

We can call him Al. It's the name he used in Belize City, and I wouldn't presume to improve upon it. Paunchy in his polo shirt, he appeared on the balcony of the Seaside Guest House and let himself into a tiny single room hardly larger than a public restroom stall. He was wearing acid-washed jeans and white tennies, and looked to be on the early edge of fifty. The day previous, the guesthouse teemed with the usual motley lot of backpackers and day-trippers: a dreadlocked Austrian, a clean-scrubbed American Mormon, a Canadian fry cook from Florida, a pair of dusty, hippie-beautiful women from the Netherlands. Now they were all gone, off to catch a bus to Guatemala, or water taxis to the Cayes. Where they had all appeared worldly and roadworthy, Al I could picture back in the States, wearing slacks and a name tag, selling home appliances in a strip mall. The others looked like they'd traveled here. Al looked like he'd been caught here.

The Seaside Guest House is run by Quakers, and it is optimistically christened. You can *smell* the sea from the second floor, if the wind is right, and should the palm leaves part to provide a sight line over the tin roofs and down the adjacent alley, you might spy a scintilla of Caribbean glint, but knock your Belikin bottle over the balcony railing and you'll ding a taxi, not a sunbather. At the far end of the balcony, two doors form a right angle. One opens into the tiny single room Al entered. The other opens on a common room furnished with a few chairs and a simple table. A hallway leads from the common area to a handful of double rooms, and at the far end, the bathroom. Just off the common area, at the head of the hall, is a bunk room crammed with six beds, one of which was mine. The bunk room and Al's room share a common wall.

Below the rooms, the first floor is taken up with a few tables, an abbreviated breakfast counter, and a small storage room. A young man named Omar mans the admissions desk. Behind Omar, in an office nook, the proprietor passes the time by reading. He is whip-thin, soft-spoken, and given to peering professorially over his half-glasses. I spoke with him the day Al arrived, and he said he taught part-time at the university. Throughout our brief conversation, he was methodically unsealing envelopes, his long fingers moving like deliberate, articulated caterpillars. The guesthouse is girded by a tall wooden fence and a locked gate that opens directly on Prince Street. Shortly after he entered his tiny room, Al reemerged, descended the stairs, let himself out the gate and disappeared down the street.

It was quiet after Al left. I sat at a table in the common area, composing notes toward a story on Belizian firefighters. When the hot breeze blew, the palms rattled like rain. Across Prince Street, a little old man, his face a wizened pecan, sat under an orange Ovaltine cap on a chair in the sun. Now and then he spoke to a woman ironing in the shade of the great white house that dominated the garden. The woman was built like an oil drum, wrapped in a vast white apron that bulged from her gut like a sail full of wind. Their soft Spanish floated across Prince Street and up through the screen.

A local reporter arrived and drove me to a seaside club, where we sat at an open-air table overlooking the water, eating chips and salsa spiked with cilantro and chunks of raw conch. At dusk, a squall kicked up and drove inland in a darkening smear. The waitstaff moved around the deck, unfurling canvas curtains as the first rain spit through. I noticed a man standing alone at the railing, hands in his pockets, faced into the wind. It was Al. At his back, disco lights swabbed the barren dance floor. When the reporter and I left, the floor had drawn a few dancers. Al was on the fringe, hanging back.

· · ·

Back in the guesthouse just after midnight, I have the six-bunk dorm room to myself. It's a cheapskate's special: the dorm room, at the dorm room rate, with no roommates—save for a beetle the size of Delaware that click-clacks across the floor when I switch the light on. I make a few notes in my journal, then settle in to sleep.

I waken some time later. Someone is fumbling with a door. Al has returned, and it sounds as if he has a friend. A woman is giggling. The wall between us is made of gapped one-inch boards; a few hairline strips of light seep through with the sound. I hear the bunk creak, hear the woman's voice. Switching between Spanish and Creole, she sounds pleasantly, lazily drunk, her voice a slurring purr. Al begins to petition her for specific favors. She giggles alcoholically, but remains firm on one point: *"Condom! Condom!"* He protests, quietly and urgently. She mentions a young daughter, asks for more tequila. I hear the bottle tip. I hear Al's voice again, and again, rather loudly this time, she insists that he produce a condom. He shushes her, but soon I hear the rattle of the wrapper. It becomes quiet. I hear weight shifting. Still no words. More sounds of movement. There is trouble. Al can't get hard. He makes another request. She demurs—"It will taste bitter." Again, he shushes her. The drinking and negotiations continue. Soon she is on a bipolar drunk, looping from coy to surly. At one of her low points, she mumbles about suicide. Then she brightens, asks for the bathroom. Al lets her in the main area, points her down the hall, then hides in his room while she pees noisily. Then I can see her reflection under my door. She is drifting around the common area. A chair creaks, and a newspaper crackles. It is quiet for a long time. Finally, Al stirs and creeps from his room. Then a harsh whisper: *"What the hell are you doing?!"* After much cajoling and shushing, he maneuvers her back to his room. But now she wants to leave. "This place is poison for me," she says. She asks if she can take the newspaper.

"Stay—I will make love to you in the morning," says Al.

"You will have to wake me up."

"I can go to your place," says Al, ever hopeful.

"My place is not so clean as this." She laughs bitterly.

"But I will be more relaxed there," says Al. The woman says nothing. Al speaks again. "Tomorrow I go to Caye Caulker. Meet me."

"Can I have cab fare?"

"No prob-lem-o." He shepherds her down the stairs and to the gate, shushing all the way. The gate clicks, and she is on her own. I hear him return to his room. I hear the condom wrapper crackle, hear him cap the tequila. Then he pads down the hall to the bathroom. My journal was on the floor beside my bunk. I've been taking notes in the dark. I press the light on my watch. It's 2:30 a.m. I'm a little guilty about the notes, but you find yourself privy to something like this, to the dialogue and circumstance of two people driven by two very different sorts of desperation, and you think you ought to turn it into some sort of parable. At the moment, I'm on my moral high horse, disgusted by a man who, unable to use her, would turn a woman loose in Belize City at this hour, leaving her to weave through the carnivorous backstreets to her sleeping baby. But the story is more complex than that. It is about the human transactions we all make, about the hungers and incompletenesses that drive us, furtive and craven, into dark places, dark places that we inhabit only so that we may buy some time in the light. Worlds apart, separated by a lamina of social, cultural, and economic stratifications, Al and the woman were put on intersecting trajectories by twinned—not twin—needs. This is a damned lonely world, and given cover of darkness, we drive straight to the things we disdain by day. We want them hidden, but more than that, we want them.

Al is still in the bathroom when she returns. She is banging at the gate. "Al! Al! Al!" The mongrel dog who lies by the desk all day, soundless and unstirring, begins barking wildly. Now she is ringing the doorbell, again and again. Doors slam below. Omar and the manager are cursing the woman, yelling at her to leave. She calls out for Al. His reflection slides past my door as he returns from the bathroom. I can feel him holding his breath as he quietly lets himself out the main door and into his room, but she has spotted him.

"Al! Al!" The lock on his door clicks in place.

Now I hear the proprietor, no longer professorial. "It's that fucking guy in Room One!" His voice moves to the foot of the stairs. "You brought her in here, buddy, now make her leave! Tell her to go home!" Al's room is dark and silent. Downstairs, the yelling and door slamming continue. Omar cracks the gate and the woman wedges her foot in the jamb. Enraged, the proprietor grabs a machete and chases her down the street, into the darkness. For a while it is quiet. Then the proprietor's voice, from the foot of the stairs again.

"If you *want* a fucking whorehouse, *go* to a fucking whorehouse!"

And then it was quiet for good.

Al was gone in the morning. I caught a ride north, figured when I got back home I'd write up the escapade as a humorous farce: "Likkered Up Hookers Ain't Nothin' but a Heartache," or some such. But it just didn't seem funny. I thought of him flying down here for hookers and snorkeling, and then I thought of me flying down here to fish for stories, a slumming voyeur armed with emergency traveler's checks and a plane ticket home, and I recognized that obscenity is relative. Scribbling away in my bunk, snuffling around the edge of this little story like a jackal just beyond the firelight, I was doing some skulking of my own. Given a front-row seat at the disintegration of one man's fantasy, I found myself reviewing my

own closeted collection of moldering ghouls and ossified in-
discretions. If they were brought to light, would I live differ-
ently, or just more defiantly?

Our passions debase us. Our needs make fools of us all.

1999

RSVP to the KKK

One morning in February of 1998, I found two
pieces of mail in my mailbox. This essay is a reply to
one of them.

◌ ◌ ◌

Dear Grand Dragon Wayne:
Received your gracious invitation to participate
in the White Pride Rally, Saturday, August 22,
in Dyess, Arkansas. I am unable to attend. In
lieu of my actual presence, please accept the
following observations and recommendations,
elicited by and culled from your flyer. Perhaps
you can share my thoughts aloud at the end of
the day when you gather 'round the flickering
embers of the cross to toast marshmallows and
let your hoods down.

First of all, your direct-mail technique is
sterling. The hand-addressed envelope, the

rubber-stamped return address, the letter-from-Grandma size envelope, all work to create an "open me" feel. While the knight-on-a-rearing-horse icon is a bit fanciful, it is balanced nicely by the no-nonsense all-caps rendering of the National Association for the Advancement of White People acronym.

As to the flyer itself, I am quite taken with the hand-drawn border, festooned as it is with disembodied cartoony hoods— very Casper the Friendly Ghost. However, I note with perplexity that you have chosen to scratch out your typos—surely any self-respecting Grand Dragon would jump at the chance to use a little Wite-Out®. You might also wish to reexamine the photocopying process, as reproductive corruption of the caricatures of Grand Wizard Ray Larsen and Public Relations man Damon Lance Rose (That name—are you sure about this guy?) causes them to appear as morose, hooded black men being kissed on the brow by a bat-winged Easter chick.

I note with relief that "<u>THIS IS A FAMILY AFFAIR!</u>" with "NO ALCOHOL, FIREARMS, DRUGS OR FIGHTING!" and "<u>WOMEN AND CHILDREN ARE MOST WELCOME</u>." I don't need to tell you, Grand Dragon Wayne, or spell it out in underlined capital letters, that this country is going to heck in a handbasket, and I well note your dedication to the preservation of the extended family. It takes a village, y'know. It is also a testament to your perspicacity that in addition to food and beverages, you will be offering souvenirs. Good thinking. From Marxism to Lilith Fair, what's a movement without merch? Modern movements also require sponsors, and I see you've been so blessed by the National Knights of the Ku Klux Klan. Congrats. I am less enchanted by the fact that I will have the opportunity to "MEET POLITICAL SPEAKERS FROM AROUND THE COUNTRY." Can't we keep politics out of this? Hell, Grand Dragon Wayne, you know you can't trust politicians. You get them involved, and before long you'll have to take a senator to dinner, fill out thirteen forms, and complete a ten-year environmental impact study just to burn one little ol' cross. The upside? When it's time to take it to the streets, your politician friends may be able to expedite the parade permit process.

I am also in receipt of the NAAWP application form. While it turns out I'm not eligible (The breakdown: native-born—yes; loyal United States Citizen—yes, by and large; white—seems like it, but I've not done my genealogy home-work, and I tan with suspicious speed and depth; temperate habits—yes, at least the ones I admit to; of Christian faith—not to your satisfaction; and, believe in White Rights and Americanism—see Christian faith), I'm intrigued by the box that says "I am a former member and would like to be rein-stated." I assume this is in compliance with your Christian faith prerequisite (forgiveness, the prodigal son, etc.), but I wonder: Will dues be prorated?

Okay, Grand Dragon Wayne, joke's over. Here's the deal. I don't curse much, but when I opened your letter in our little post office, the temperature in my gut dropped twenty degrees and I said something very nasty indeed. Your sentiments slithered right into my tiny hometown, right into my mailbox, right into my hand. That disturbs me. Did you think I was some sort of Aryan rough boy? From the way you addressed my letter I can tell you got my name from a series of articles I wrote for a working-class magazine. One on a country music star and his gun store. One on snowmobile racing. And one on monster trucks. Apparently I fit your recruitment profile. You must have missed my piece on the contributions of black artists to country music.

Well, Grand Dragon, it's true that no one will mistake me for an Ivy League–educated liberal professor of multicultural studies any time soon. I hunt. I own guns. I own my share of camouflage clothing. I'm a loner. I shave infrequently. My transport of choice is a beat-up pickup truck. I've been known to sing old country music songs at the top of my lungs with no trace of irony. I know my way around the woods at night, and harbor a touch of disdain for anyone who doesn't. But don't save me a beer at the rally.

I despise you, but in a more complex way than you might suspect.

I despise you not just because you are a racist, but because you obscure the true complexities of racism and serve as an easy out for anyone seeking superficial absolution. You are frightening, Grand Dragon Wayne, and you are dangerous, but you are out in the open. In a country hung up on skin, you are the equivalent of a wart—unattractive, perhaps even precancerous, but easily identifiable, and, if need be, easily removed.

Meanwhile, the real problems facing us are much more in the character of a metastatic melanoma—a deadly malignancy with tendrils that lace the entire substructure of society. Your type serves as a lightning rod to divert our focus from the deeply insidious nature of prejudice and racism. We get you on *Jerry Springer*, make fun of your hood, shout you down, engage in group behavior the equivalent of poking a dumb animal with a stick, and then, having solved nothing, hit the remote feeling a self-congratulatory shot of vindication. Meanwhile, you head home too much the true believer to be humiliated, and likely having made a convert or two. Thinking we know who's to fear and who's to blame, we stop questioning. If racism were woven with a thread as pure as your white sheet, stripping it out would be a simple matter indeed. Unfortunately it is woven in all shades. In fine, delicate strands. And it is interracial as hell. It is as blatant as spray-painted epithets and as subtle as an averted gaze. It storms through the streets, but even more frequently it coasts through the suburbs in a minivan. It thwarts human endeavor, it plays both ways, it is used as leverage, it is roundly ignored. Its greatest toll is exacted not through white-hot hate, but through distrust and sadness.

I also despise you because you remind me that we live in a world where bumper stickers pass for intelligent discourse, Grand Dragon Wayne. You've seen them: "You Can't Hug Your Children With Nuclear Arms." "When Guns Are Outlawed, Only Outlaws Will Have Guns." "Think Globally, Act Locally." "Mean People Suck." "I'm [insert indignant term here] and I Vote." Etc., and yaddety. None of these one-dimensional aphorisms stand up well under examination, and I remain suspicious of anyone who can express their most deeply held convictions in the space of a bumper sticker. But that's the way we've come to deal with things. Pick out the obvious, yell at or about it, and click off the remote feeling self-righteous. No heavy lifting required.

Simply railing at you is like displaying a bumper sticker—it makes me feel better, looks good to my assumed constituency, but accomplishes little in the big picture. There is enough disingenuous behavior on both sides of the race issue to suggest that the true path to reconciliation can only happen on a personal level, one to one. So I'm taking this personally, Grand Dragon Wayne. You and me. I hope to undermine you by taking your invitation, making fun of it in public, and then, more importantly, pointing out that as nasty as you are, you are only a marginal, distracting symptom of a systemic problem.

A guy like me, Wayne, I pay the rent by writing, a little piece about monster trucks here, and essay about the joys of summer there, all the while hoping I'll have a chance to write something of greater importance someday. You've given me that chance, and I'm taking it. But I don't mind telling you the fact that you know where I live frightens me. The fact that you sat down with a pen and wrote my name and hometown on an envelope makes me want to stay away from windows.

Do y' like irony, Grand Dragon Wayne? Hope so, because then you'll love this: When I found that envelope in my mail-box, it was nestled cheek-to-cheek with a letter from the Southern Poverty Law Center. They were asking me to sup-port their "Teaching Tolerance" program. To take their "Tol-erance Challenge," and "say 'yes' to tolerance." I admit I'm reminded of the bumper stickers. And their envelope was a mass-mailing job; no handwritten address. They probably don't even know where I live. But I think I'll send 'em a little something. Your name and address, for one thing.

Have a nice summer.

1998

People to Avoid on the
Backpack Circuit

I've seen a bunch of territory with my backpack right
behind me. Fifteen or sixteen countries, something
like that. One winter, I moseyed around Central America. Actually, I went to Belize for two weeks, but it
sounds so much more intriguing to say Central America. Conjures up visions of revolution, drug smuggling,
and Harrison Ford. Anyway, I had my backpack, and I
ran into some other folks with backpacks, and soon I
began to notice things. Those things are listed below.

○ ○ ○

So you've decided to stuff your life in a rein-
forced nylon box and hoof it for hostel
world—travel by foot and thumb, amble the
back roads with nary a care, nary a plan, nary a
feeling in your arms, the straps are digging in
that hard. But be forewarned: tribulation (and

a permanent subscapular cramp the size of a volleyball) awaits the backpacker! Never mind the wild-eyed street hustlers, the crack-addled pickpockets or the Kalashnikov-toting teenage border guards. They may chase you down the street, finger your lint, or confiscate your passport and string you up by the thumbs, but they'll rarely stand on your face to reach the top bunk, prattle on until 3 a.m. about the meaning of life and a psychic aunt in Des Moines, or throw up on your sleeping bag— unlike your fellow travelers, classified and listed as follows:

THE LONG-SKIRTED EARTH MOTHER   A vastly patient spirit. Speaks in the earnest monotones of a third-rate folk singer reciting a poem written by a third-grader about a dead dog. Likely to trigger repressed memories of support groups and bad incense. Certain to be outfitted with a handmade Guatemalan tote bag. Finds wonder in all things. Badgers you to accept a copy of a cancer-curing plantain poultice recipe channeled to her in a daydream by an eighth-century Mayan faith healer. Look, lady, I'll sort my cans, I'll cut back on the beef, and I'll even hang a dream catcher from the rearview mirror, but in the meantime aren't you late for a harmonic convergence somewhere?

THE "WHERE-THE-HELL'S McDONALD'S?" GUY   Say no more. More than likely, there's a backward baseball cap involved.

RICH KIDS WITH GEAR   A particularly revolting strain of happy camper. Usually reeking with an air of self-sacrifice, positively edematous with pride over their willingness to mingle with quaint third world beggar types. Generally packing things like miniature triple-locking machine-knurled aquamarine carabiner keychains, portable campfire espresso maker with brass steam pipe and oscillating rescue strobe, and fully digital titanium insect repellent dispensers. "Look, Mummy— it's got 100% DEET!"

THE BOOBS OF BERLITZ   These are people determined to inflict their hack native tongue despite the native's desire to communicate in English, in which the native has been fluent since the age of three. The Boobs of Berlitz are easily recognized. They generally walk around with their finger stuck up their phrase book.

MULTILINGUAL, HISTORICALLY AND GEOGRAPHICALLY INFORMED EUROPEANS These people make you feel ignorant and inferior. As well they should.

Now then. Excoriating these folks without affording them the opportunity to defend themselves is hardly sporting. But it is certainly good fun. To prevent my completely alienating anyone who ever hoisted a pack, however, I reckon it prudent that I answer the question, "OK, Mr. Crabby Pants, where do you fit on the list?" And then I must admit that at any given time, I can be placed in nearly all of the above categories. I mean, I'm no earth mother, but on a recent backpacking trip to Belize, I did pack a tube of camper's biodegradable soap. Great stuff. Smells like coconuts. Gives you that fresh, clean feeling, as if you've been scrubbed with . . . coconuts. As far as the McDonald's guy, well, I was doing just great, eating nothing but jungle rat and unidentified tubers, until that lonely afternoon in Orange Walk Town when I spotted a woman selling Snickers bars. . . . And I'm certainly no rich kid, but I do have gadget disease. Got me a portable water purifier before I left. Aw, it's great. Top o' the line. Fits right in the backpack. Tubes, plungers, little hoses, charcoal filters, the works. This thing would separate Rush Limbaugh from a box of chocolates. Of course it never came out of the box. They may be a third world country, but they got bottled water. I don't carry phrase books, so I'm not really a Berlitz boob, but I did once spend five minutes dancing around a small post office in rural Germany, holding a postcard in my teeth, flapping my arms and saying "luft!" over and over. Eventually the postmistress looked at me and said, "Air Mail?"

Which brings me back to those self-satisfied, smug Europeans. That's the one group in which I can't claim membership. But I expect the look of smug will soon be replaced by the look of mouth breather. On what do I construct my thesis? Why, the fact that the most popular television show in Europe is . . . *Baywatch*. For the moment, they're multilingual. But when we get done implanting Pamela Anderson in their national semi-consciousness, I expect their love of language, history and culture will rapidly devolve into monosyllabic ruminations on reruns. And then, finally, there will exist among the tromping ranks of backpacking a subgroup that we can approach without trepidation and compare subscapular cramps.

1996

○ ○ ○

P.S. Again, I retract the Limbaugh comment, for reasons already stated on page 49. It may be of anecdotal interest that at one time I was paid roughly $6.50 an hour to listen to Rush Limbaugh. If you're keeping track, that's just under twenty bucks a day. It was 1992, and my employer was an overbusy conservative who wanted to know what all the fuss was about. I'd listen to the car radio in the parking lot and report back. Frankly, Rush was funnier back then.

I recently backpacked out of the Grand Canyon following a six-day river trip. My day pack felt a tad heavy. Having made the 4,400-foot climb out of Bright Angel Trail, I discovered that some wise guy had hidden a five-pound rock beneath my gorp baggie. A well-executed practical joke is a thing of beauty, and I laughed out loud. That said, I have compiled a list of suspects. Time is on my side. . . .

Falling Together

An elderly woman has fallen in the street. It is London, noon, rush hour. She lands violently, on her buttocks and elbows, her head snapping back on impact. Her capacious white poke of a purse pinwheels across the zebra crossing, spitting handkerchiefs, pill bottles, a compact, pens, bits of paper, a trove of clutter. Thirty yards up the road, the traffic light switches to green, releasing a horde of small cars. The purse slides to a halt, bright and gaping in the sun, the white plastic brilliant against the oily tarmac. The cars surge forward, toward the old woman.

Seated in the upper level of a double-decker bus stopped at a light, I'm looking down on traffic. The bus is enclosed, a sleek, soulless version of the classic red double-decker. A morning of unrelenting sun has turned it into a rolling hothouse. Several passengers are smoking; the smoke and the sun have worked behind my eyes, and the inklings of a headache have begun to seep through my temples. I'm tracking the cars and considering sleep when the flash of the white spinning purse catches my eye. The woman next to me squawks and whips on point like a weathervane, her arm extended stiffly, index finger waggling. The old woman is just off the front of the bus and in the opposite lane. Her cheerfully patterned dress has flown above her waist, revealing doughy thighs and gray cotton underpants. But she has seen the cars, and her fear eclipses her mortification. Weeping and screaming, she claws at the sky, her fingers splayed and crooked, as if she hopes to hook the air and find her feet. The cars are gaining speed. She kicks a leg straight, and a shoe flips loose, arcing up and over her head, then skittering to the gutter. The heel is broken, set at an unnatural cant, like a dislocated thumb. On the bus, the passengers are on their feet. They gasp and ogle, bump shoulders for a clearer view.

An old man lurches from the curb, running to the woman with herky-jerky steps, as if he is on the strings of a palsied puppeteer. His loose brown pants flap at his shins. He bends stiffly, at the hips and knees, and reaches both hands to the woman. His eyes are wide, his fingers set to trembling so violently I can see them flutter from the bus. His jaw is working, his mouth springing open and closed as if he has a tongueful of hot food. The couple's hands meet and clasp, the old man tugs and shuffles backward. She is nearly upright when his grip fails, and she crashes back to the pavement.

I find myself rising from my seat, intent on disembarking. I will flag traffic. Pull the woman to safety. Put an arm around the old man's shoulders, lead him safely to the curb. The thoughts are reflex, and I am just off the cushions when the bus lumbers ahead and the woman is cut from view. On my feet now, I crane my neck with everyone else, and see only the pack of cars, their headlong charge unabated. Two blocks farther on, someone flags the toothy hospitality woman and orders tea in a paper cup. The sun is tropical. Ten minutes later, I doze.

Ten years later. I am passing through London and think of the old woman. I would like to think the cars stopped. Perhaps they didn't stop. Perhaps they did stop, but in the fall she broke a hip, and her husband came to the hospital room holding miniature daffodils cut from their garden. Perhaps she never went home again. Her story is part of my story, but in my story, her story ends without conclusion.

If you accept that time is linear, and that we are propelled by time, it follows that life is a proposal of position and momentum, and that we are continuously hurtling through an infinite bristle of convergence. Yesterday I folded cilantro into a venison stir fry using a spatula hewn from a tapered strip of birch. It was carved by an old man in Norway. We met briefly over a small dinner in his sister's garden. He spoke only Norwegian. Taking his leave, he simply handed me the spatula and smiled. I knew seven phonetically memorized Norwegian words, and used three of them: *"Monge tusen takk"*—many thousand thanks. A decade later, I bring out the spatula several times a week. I stir water chestnuts and thyme, and wonder if the old man still lives.

One need not leave the La-Z-Boy, much less ride a bus through London or hitchhike across Norway, to transect a fragment of drama or intimacy. Like the actors in Luis Buñuel's *The Phantom of Liberty*, we are simply Brownian particles made flesh, following a fractured arc defined as much by chaos as purpose. But when we wander, when we step outside the familiar, by choice or by chance, the reductive powers of displacement effect a distillation that casts distinct events in sharp relief. The old woman's tragedy becomes mythic; unable to reach her, I leave her forever in the street, forever before the onrushing traffic. The old man's spatula becomes totemic; passed from his hand to mine, it represents the intimate, fleeting points of intersection we find only on the wander.

Shedding the mundane everyday, and moving, always moving, the wanderer experiences a constant juxtaposition of intimacy and transience that produces a chronology of focal points to which we anchor distinct moments in time. An old woman falls and screams, and shows me the primal soul of her. An old man hands me a blade of wood and I cook with it forever. We share an intimacy far exceeding the intimacy I feel for people I see daily.

Sleeping under a small tent in the outskirts of Budapest just before the fall of communism, I was awakened after midnight by a thief kneeling on my feet. I remember the darkness, and the sound of his fingers rustling through my backpack, his breath as he leaned above me, and I remember the fear that flash-froze my guts. My first thought was of home. Then I rared up and drove my fist into his face. He rolled backward out the tent, and I heard his feet pound away in the dark. I wonder about the thief sometimes, who he might have been, what he might have intended, and how it is that we came to converge, as close as skin on skin, linked forever, even as we ricochet away at the speed of time.

1999

Branding God

Throughout my childhood and young adulthood, "going to church" meant going to someone's home on Sunday morning and gathering quietly in the living room. We prayed, sang a few austere a cappella hymns and read verses from the Bible before offering up brief, homemade homilies. You could usually smell a roast simmering in the kitchen adjacent. There was deep comfort in the quiet assemblage.

When I was sixteen, I began a five-year stint working on a Wyoming ranch run by a family of my same religion. I didn't know it then, but I was taking the first steps on a skeptic's journey. Today, I can no longer believe as I once did. But I am no bitter heretic. The people in this story, the people I met with for an entire childhood of Sunday mornings, the parents who raised and taught me in love, are people whom, quite simply and profoundly, I owe.

♡ ♡ ♡

Brother Tim Copper was preaching brimstone, and God Himself was bringing the backbeat. We were gathered in a long, empty, quonset-style granary, seated on wooden benches, receiving the Word. All around the granary, wheat fields stretched away for miles. Brother Tim was working Revelations, if my recollection is correct—and it might not be, I had my eye on this particular girl—and the Good Lord was working a towering thunder bank just off to the southwest, sliding it in on golden shafts of setting sun and legs of lightning, all the while staccato-dancing his fingers across a kettle-drum forged in the storms of Jupiter. The hot wind pushed sweet rain-a-comin' dust under the granary door and set the ladies' skirts to stirring. Bible pages riffled, and the young girls put their hands to their hair lest it come unpinned. Brother Tim had Revelations, he had the terrible, swift sword a-flashing from the sky, and he had the admonitory thunder. He had the groove.

I'll give him this: He knew how to work it. The nearer that storm drew, the more the wind made the roofing nails squawk and the tin roof retch, the taller he rose, glowering from the plywood riser, squeezing the Word in one hand, index finger bookmarking verses he knew by rote. His perfervid eyes swept the congregation like a shark working a beach. This was no come to the warm and sheltering bosom of Christ speech, this was an operatic Armageddon rafter rattler. Brother Tim was recommending Heaven by pointing the way to Hell, double-timing our sorry souls like a drill instructor assigned a platoon of pudgy mollycoddles. The march was on, he said, lag behind and be damned. We trembled with truth.

We weren't used to this sort of thing. Our Sunday meetings were hushed, reverent affairs, parsed with sotto voce prayer, subdued testimony, and muted hymns. Even for this, the Saturday night service of our yearly convention, a service in which the meeting is typically "tested" at the conclusion to see if anyone will stand and silently profess their willingness to walk with God, the thunder from the dais was unexpected and unusual. Even I, distracted as I was by the young nursing student two rows forward and one bench down, found myself caught up in the terrible power of the whole thing, moved by the cinematics of it all: Brother Tim's bituminous eyes, his portentous certainty, the way he seemed to summon thunder each time he punched the air with his Bible. It was as if Wagner's Valkyries had dropped in on the Quakers.

I *don't go* to church anymore. I was a young cowboy then, working summers on a ranch in Wyoming. Six days a week we worked, with Sunday a strictly observed day of rest. Sunday came from another world. We sat through meeting reverent in our clean socks and stiff boots, then lazed in the cool bunkhouses or fiddled around down by the river. Out by the shop, the equipment that smoked and roared all week sat silent. I used to stand among the tools on the cool concrete and look out through the greasy glass panes over the grinder and marvel at the way the ranch changed on its day off. A permeant placidity settled over everything, from the woodchucks sunning on the junk piles to the tall grass waving easy on the plateau above the river. Today, an afternoon seems constrained, only a matter of hours. Then, on a Sunday, time was expansive, gracious, accommodating. One Sunday, after meeting had drawn to a close and we had returned our Bibles to our bunkhouses, we gathered in the cookhouse for dinner. I remember roast beef and gravy, but then that would be a fairly safe bet. The women had a little extra bustle about them this Sunday, because brother Tim Copper was at the table. In our little corner of Wyoming, Brother Tim was seen as the heavyweight champ of preaching. Church members would grin and shake their heads in benevolent wonder when recounting his exploits; the deeper implication was that he was not to be messed with. Preaching or not, Brother Tim tended to Hold Forth. This day he was in strong, confident voice, sharing the stories of sinners and their weakness in the face of salvation. There was a woman nearby who had been coming to church off and on for some time. She was a beautiful thing, and, as the story went, had worked as a model. We heard anecdotes of her struggle, of her inability to adhere to our dress code, for which women are forbidden to cut their hair or wear pants. After working with her for some time, with mixed success, Tim paid her a surprise visit. She answered the door in a pair of shorts. By his own account, Brother Tim spun on his heel, walked right back out the sidewalk to his car, and drove away. The woman who first told me this story chuckled with admiration for Tim's resolve. But the chuckle was double-edged; it also conveyed condescending pity for this woman who didn't know enough to slip into a skirt and save her soul.

The idea of an unannounced inspection struck me as goofy as it was creepy. But that paled in comparison to the idea of this man filled with such vindictive hubris that he was willing to risk this woman's soul to Hell, to abandon her in her own home, willing to stand before the throne of God on the Big Day and say, Lord, she was clad in shorts, so I turned away. I got her behind me, back there with Satan.

I can still see him, down at the south end of the long cook-house table, right across from me, his big frame backlit in the window, telling this story with booming certitude, and I remember thinking, if the kingdom of heaven can swing on a pair of hot pants, if the cut of your shorts can shift the firmament, then we got trouble. And now, when I think back, I feel a little sorry for him, sad that he could tell these stories in front of a kid like me and not have any perception of my perception. Blown up in his own spiritual bulk, he unwittingly blocked the one true light, and a shadow fell on my heart. In time, I came to know others like Tim Copper. In their zeal to count heads, they lost track of souls. And when they saw some of us turn away, they assumed we simply strayed, or were tempted away, or left in ignorance, when in truth, many of us left in full awareness, seeking a purer truth. He wasn't the only one. But I remember that Sunday. For the first time, I felt the foundation of my faith crack.

On Mondays, we left the Sunday world, and dove back into work. In the weeks leading up to Brother Tim's gospel in the granary, we had been branding. Branding days usually began with a roundup. Understand: When I showed up at the Double 8 Ranch in Elk Mountain, Wyoming, I was no cowboy. I was wearing blue corduroy pants and a flowered disco shirt. It was only my second-favorite disco shirt, but it had flowers on it, and I figured these ranchers I was meeting would be more receptive to flowers than the jarring black and orange geometrics of my number-one favorite disco shirt. I was sixteen, and I had ideas about these things.

I had never ridden a horse. Well, I had, but never really on my own, or to any useful end. There was this neighbor girl once, she was eighteen, I was twelve or so, and I had for her a saturating case of puppy love, and once, at the pitch of my fever, she gave me a ride on her horse. I remember tingling and trying not to tremble, or trembling and trying not to tingle, and I remember acting desperately nonchalant, but I do not remember the horse, except that I suppose it might have been brown. Then my friend Reno Norsk had a pony named

Daisy. He brought her over one day and shared his thermos of sugary iced tea and we rode her out to the swamp, and, because we had heard high schoolers talking about it, we got naked and went streaking. A buddy from high school, George Brux, whom I always remember fondly when I look at the disfigured half-moon under the nail of my right index finger— he flattened it with a racquetball racquet—sent me out on his horse once, and I should have known better, because Georgie was one gleefully sadistic cat, and before it was over the horse was on a runaway. I was dangling by one leg and one arm, just like a movie Indian attacking a Conestoga. I don't remember how we got the horse stopped, but I remember Georgie cackling maniacally. My grandpa had horses; I think he might have taken me for a ride once. And I had this high school girlfriend for a while, we'd ride double out into the moonlight, the horse's hooves whispering through the damp alfalfa, and I'd murmur in her ear and keep my arms around her, and we wafted from one Teen Romance Hall of Fame moment to another, until I reached to open a gate, slid from behind the saddle and landed flat on my back, where I lay gasping like a guppy in the Gobi.

The point is, when I showed up at the Double 8, my horse-riding skills were those of an Eskimo hairdresser. I got away with this for the first two years, since I was only on hire for the haying season. But the third year I came out early for branding season and had to saddle up with the real hands. I learned how to put the saddle blanket on, checking it for any burrs or wrinkles that might cause a saddle sore. I learned about bridles and hackamores, and how to trick a horse into accepting the bit. I was given a saddle, and learned how to cinch it up and strap it down. Some horses fight the cinch, huff up full of air, holding it until you're done, hoping you won't notice. Then they exhale and leave the cinch dangerously slack. When you catch a horse doing this, you knee them in the belly, hard, and when they woof out the air, you snub that cinch up snug as a barrel strap.

I learned, but I just never felt comfortable around horses. For one thing, the other cowboys had been doing this all their lives, and it was impossible for me to replicate their natural ease. They'd see me being tentative, and one of them would say something about acting smarter than the horse. Don't let them know you're afraid of them, that sort of thing. Which is fine, unless you're afraid of them. And I was. Not in a skittery, weak-Willy way, but in a contemplative *My, look at the size of those murderous hocks* way. I grew up around giant Holstein cows, including ones that tried to kick me when I milked them, but acting smarter than a milk cow and acting smarter than a horse are completely separate propositions. And horses, they always look at you with a certain malevolent disdain. Even when you're up in the saddle, reins firmly in hand, a horse can emit palpable rays of contempt simply by adjusting the angle of its ears. They're faster than we, they're sleeker than we, they're hung better than we, and they seem to know it.

In a way, I'm short-selling myself. In all my years on the ranch, I was never bucked off, and I did ride some buckers. Well, one. I learned to slouch into the sway when the horses were walking, I learned how to ride the every-other hippity-bippity groove of a horse on the trot, and I loved to cut out across the prairie after a galloping stray. And my proudest achievement? I never—*never*—grabbed the saddle horn when things got dicey. Only a nancy greenhorn grabs the saddle horn, and I would have sacrificed my sacroiliac before I'd have grabbed the saddle horn in front of all those real cowboys. Of course, it helped that I spent the bulk of my horseback time aboard a one-eyed ball of fire named Cisco.

Cisco was held in reserve for amateurs. He had the disposition of a cranky tortoise, meaning he sustained all the haughty nature of his equine peers, without the sudden moves. I could do just about anything—sneeze, drop my reins or hat—and he would remain stoic, waiting patiently for the incompetent nincompoop on his back to gather up his gear. Apart from the one nonfunctioning walleye, he was in generally good health, and able to perform passably—albeit perfunctorily—in the field. At least, he was able to perform up to the standards I set. I came to feel a measure of affection for Cisco over the years, and even though I knew I was astride the official horse with training wheels, it didn't stop me from slouching and squinting just like all the other cowboys as we headed up the meadow each day to gather the day's branding stock. I may have been riding with training wheels, but by heck, I was riding.

Then came graduation day. Someone else showed up whose horse-riding abilities were worse than mine. As I recall, it was some fair-skinned citified friend of the family on a lark. "What'll we do with Mike?" asked the boss's son. "Put 'im on Warts," said the boss.

My boss, Pres, the sawed-off, jut-jawed personification of a dyspeptic banty rooster, was a solid and fair man, but he possessed a lurking wild-eyed temper accessed by a fuse shorter than his little bowlegs. When the fuse lit, he was prone to sputtering, high-octane tirades. His anger burned bright, but it burned brief. There would be an explosion, a lovely pyrotechnic spray with plenty of *boom-boom-boom*, and then, just as quickly, silence—the better in which to contemplate the reverberations of his declarations. "Put 'im on Warts," he said, and the adventure began. Warts was a good bit taller than Cisco, lean and deep chestnut brown, and the minute I stepped beside her in the stall, her ears flattened and she began emitting palpable contempt rays. No one told me at the time, but Warts was a head-tosser. That is, in addition to saddle and bridle, she required a piece of equipment, called a tie-down, that ran from her chin to her chest. Without the tie-down, she responded to the reins by tossing her head in the air and shaking her neck. Without the tie-down, she was unsteerable and unstoppable. When I saddled up, I left the tie-down hanging on the tack-room wall.

I led Warts out the stable door, where all the other cowboys and horses were gathered. Several of the hands were fussing over Cisco and the city slicker. I smiled indulgently. No more tenderfoot pony rides for me. Let the Boy Scouts ride that old bag of bones. I tightened the cinch and squinted against the sun. I'm a cowpuncher, baby. I'm a bona fide, rootin'-tootin' brushpopper on a rootin' tootin' brushpoppin' mo-chine. With one last smug glance at the pasty tourist, I swung aboard.

Perhaps I should say swung halfway aboard. For as it turned out, my bona fide, rootin'-tootin' brushpoppin' mo-chine was actually a bona fide, rootin'-tootin' rocket sled. Just as my foot was about to clear the saddle, that horse ignited.

I've seen drag racing cars that can throw fire thirty feet into the air and burn rubber halfway down a quarter-mile track—this horse made them look like a Rambler with bad clutch plates. My head snapped back, my adrenal glands liquefacted, and my life may have flashed before my eyes, but I couldn't be sure, since the calving shed flashed past at the same time. I sawed on the reins as if I were trying to bring a stampeding water buffalo to heel: Warts just tossed her head back and grabbed another gear. All across that rock-studded field, I sawed, and that horse speed-shifted—whinnying, tossing her head and shaking her mane like Lady Godiva sprinting through boot camp. We just kept gaining speed. I began to imagine I could see a cusp of air before us, bending and whitening as we pushed toward the speed of sound.

And then I saw the fence. Dead ahead, strung high and tight—an endless stretch of five-foot-high barbwire. Warts was on course for impact, and showed no signs of slowing. If she hit the fence, she'd be lacerated horribly. I'd probably be thrown clear, but would collect my own unique set of deceleration injuries, the type incurred when one terminates atmospheric reentry with a headfirst dive into an assortment of tortoise-sized boulders. If she jumped the fence, my end result would likely remain unchanged. And so I took a stupendous breath, slammed my heels into the stirrups, and reared back on the reins like a man trying to shift the Sphinx. If I had yanked on those reins any harder, that horse and I would have journeyed backward in time. The rocks flew, the grass came loose in great clods, and that nag turned her truck around in the space it would take a tree toad to tap-dance.

And shot back across the pasture like an asteroid.

I don't remember much about the trip back. Except for the part about did I have clean underwear on, and if you scream will a horse detect fear? I couldn't see too well, as we were roaring right back through the vapor trail we left on the way out. Next thing I remember we skidded smack into the middle of Pres and the rest of the crew. Somebody grabbed the bridle, and somebody grabbed a stirrup. I grabbed my chest. Pres ran to my side, reaching up to help me down. *"Get that boy down offa there!"* he yelled. Of course he's upset, I thought. He nearly lost his best hand. *"He's a-gonna ruin that dang horse!"*

I say I left the church, but I suppose the departure is necessarily incomplete. My Christian upbringing provides me with a foundation, I suppose, or a sort of sketchy paradigm, but the shining certainties are long gone, corrupted by details. We finance our journey for truth by pawning off our purities, using the wages of sin to purchase insights unavailable to those who choose to remain cloaked in the robes of the true believer. I'm not fool enough to think I've discovered truth. I know better than to rely on my interpretation of anything, be it the gospel or the weather or *Sergeant Pepper's.* I talk about the search for truth, but it is a fool's pursuit. The more you look, the less you know, to paraphrase Lao-tzu. My travels have shown me so many believers—leftists, rightists, Buddhists, Muslims, televangelists, crystal worshipers, and so on—and shown me how many of these same people are sincere and kind and misguided and difficult, that I am left spiritually schizophrenic. There is only one truth, and it is infinitely complex.

Nothing was complex in the granary that hot, late-June evening. There was Brother Tim and the one thunderous truth, and there was a brown-eyed girl two rows over. Two choices. Brother Tim had the stage, and the sound system, and the raging heavens, but that girl had just the breath of a ringlet furled at the lobe of her left ear, and lips like twin strips of silk. I looked at Tim, and for the first time I can recall, realized that all that thunder might just be thunder. I looked at that girl and I saw gentleness, and peace, and the hint of a smile, and I looked back at Tim and I saw bluster and thought maybe he'd soon be belching molten slag, and all I could think of is how that girl's hand would feel in mine. We'd been sneaking around a little bit already. The night before we'd watched the sun set over the peaks of Sybille Canyon, which were fifty miles away but still visible across the Chugwater Flats. According to local lore, the name Chugwater dated back to the time when Native Americans stampeded buffalo over a nearby cliff into a stream below. The buffalo hit the water with a *chug*. I don't know if the story is true. Someone showed me the cliff once.

The girl was half Native American. It never occurred to me to ask from which tribe. She was smart, and delicate, and strong. Later, when she married a jet engine mechanic in Kansas six months after our last date, I wrote horribly adoring poetry about her, filled with hackneyed references to her ethnicity, including made-up names intended to sound Native American. Horrendous. Verses about her "keeping a tepee with another paleface," equating her "braided raven strands" to a headdress and her denim tennies to moccasins, and lines

casting her as "cousin to the wind." Yikes. But tonight everything was poetic on its own, thick with color and possibility.
That hunger-making wind kept pushing under the door, and
through the rectangular window panels I could see miles of
wheat, orange-drenched and sinuous beneath the billowing
octopus-ink sky, the fat gusts pressing the full heads down,
making them bow and sway like a vast tribe of slim, trancing
pagans.

Still, there was drama within the clean-swept granary as
well. Because Brother Tim was winding things up. And because it was Saturday night, he'd be testing the meeting. This
is when you find out if the Lord has been moving about in the
unsaved souls of the assembled. Brother Tim had laid it all
out, let us know what we were in for, and now he would give
those who hadn't yet made their choice the opportunity to
leave the wickedness of the world—and hot pants—behind.
Toward the end of his sermon, he toned it down, became a
bit more cajoling. I can't quote him, it's been too long. But
having vividly detailed the twists and turns of the path to
Hell, having tripped through the nooks and crannies of the
fiery pit, he now made a counteroffer. Avoid all this, he said,
find your shelter in the Lord, simply by standing to your feet
on the last verse of our closing hymn. Make the choice for
Christ, choose to walk in the path of righteousness, so that
when that final day comes, you will be chosen to stand at the
right hand of God.

The place gets electric when the meetings are tested. Grown men shake and weep. Brash youths rise to their feet, faces stained with tears, their souls positively naked with holy humiliation. The buildup to that final verse is unbearable. Even thinking about it now, my chest gets light and edgy, and my pulse lifts. All that preaching, and then, in the space of six or so a cappella lines, you find out if any of it took. We finished the chorus, headed into the first lines. Heads swivel. Has anyone risen? Brother Tim lifts his eyes from his hymnal, sweeps the crowd as he did before, only now his eyes have cooled. Heat replaced with hope. The singing falls off a bit, what with everyone rubbernecking, but comes right back. No one is standing. Brother Tim keeps singing and searching. The words scale by and he becomes more furtive, more desperate. There are no histrionics, just subtle shadings. And this isn't about his ego. I believe his fear is true; he doesn't fear that his tour de force will go unrewarded, he fears that souls are being lost. The verse is drawing to a close. We're headed for the final chorus. Eternal salvation, going once, going twice . . .

If you want to look good at a branding, you got to have yourself a good heeler man. You got to know that when you arch your back, flip that dogie and free-fall to your knees bear-hugging two hundred pounds of bawling, head-butting bull calf, somewhere in there your heeler shot his arm out, snapped his fingers shut on the calf's left rear hoof, yanked straight back with all he had, and hit the dirt butt-first, with his left foot jammed in the back of the calf's right hamhock, driving it forward so the two legs form a splayed V. Meanwhile, the horse at the other end of the lariat should maintain a steady pull, keeping the loop taut. If the heeler does his job, and if the cowboy on the horse does his, their opposing efforts should anchor the calf between them. Either one lets up, you've got yourself a frantic lapful of beef, thrashing like a bathtub-sized trout with hooves. And if you are timid, or tentative, if you don't dive into that calf like you're twisting up and taking down a speed-freaked halfback, you'll find yourself flat on your back, tasting hot tooth chips and tonguing the gouge in your cheek.

It's a sweaty, smoky, stinky business, branding. It's like football without pads, it's like wrassling in high-heeled shoes. It's hard on cows, hard on cowboys, and hard on animal-rights activists. It is a noisy spectacle in an unforgiving arena. And when you're a kid among strangers, it's a test you can't walk away from. All those cowboys, all that creased leather, the noise, the smoke, your only option would be to walk off into the sagebrush, and then where would you go? Back to your bunk? Out to the dusty county road, to stick out your thumb, catch a ride to the interstate? Nope, you grab the rope and get in there.

I'm a header. I wear one leather glove on my right hand, and when the horse comes at me, towing a bawling calf, I slip past the horse's right flank, dipping in behind the stirrup, and grab the rope—stiff and rough as a frayed oak branch— loosely in my right hand. Stepping quickly now, I run my hand down its taut length until my fist snubs up against the calf's neck. The minute my fist hits, I swing my hips up against the calf's rib cage, reach my left arm across and over the calf's burred spine and down to the left flank, grab the web of skin between the abdomen and upper leg and then hoist. It all has to happen at once: Hoist, bend your back, lift straight up with both hands, knee the beast skyward and then, with a tug at the left flank, roll the calf a quarter turn in midair, laying him out flat so when we hit the dirt the left side will be exposed to the branding iron. Everything has to happen in one fluid motion. Any break in the momentum and the calf will kick free.

People can get hurt if a calf breaks loose. We work in three or four clumps, usually with our heads down and our backs turned. In the midst of all the heat and dust and noise, men are running from clump to clump handling knives, syringes and glowing branding irons. A rack of extra irons heats in an open flame. Horses work in and out of the groups, and although they're seasoned, a calf stampeding their underbelly can still cause pandemonium. And so the header and the heeler learn to work together, learn to perform this rough work like two dancers reenacting a mugging. Drop the calf, twist its head back on its neck, flip the lasso free, and hang on until the branding iron arrives.

I think I can still throw a calf. Putting a brand on God is tougher. And what do I believe? I believe Jean Cocteau was on to something when he said there are truths that one can only say after having won the right to say them. I have to believe that, because that has been my path. I believe that the search for truth follows an arc. You begin with the simple truth of ignorance, proceed to the baffling truth of complexity, and then, perhaps not until after death, end your journey with the true truth—the truth of clarity. I'm not sure the truth of clarity is available on this earth. I've met some who claim it, but they often speak not in terms of struggle but of revelation, and I am suspicious. I suspect they have taken a shortcut, cutting across from the beginning of the arc to the end. In all likelihood, they overshot, and are right back at the beginning, just in a different shade. Very little in this life is simply revealed. There is usually digging and heavy lifting involved, or some falling down. Winning—in Cocteau's terms—is costly. In the battle for my soul, I believe I won the right to some truth, but may have lost the right to redemption. Or is redemption yet available? I hope so. I pray for it, am desperate for it. Peace, grace, a fresh start . . . how I long for them in the dark hours. It is the great irony of spiritual progression: When I had peace, I didn't need it; now that I do, I can't find it. And yes, I've gone back for a look, but it's not where I left it. I read Emerson too late: "God offers to every mind its choice between truth and repose. Take which you please; you can never have both."

So what lies beyond this troubled life? Heaven? Who can say? Residual faith—hanging in threads from the ghostly paradigm—tells me death leads to some type of sorting, but perhaps not. If there's nothing, there's nothing. If there's punishment, get on with it. If there's redemption, well, humble hallelujahs. If we can customize heaven, I'll place my order now: a beat-up truck, an endless back road, and Lord, a clear conscience.

I assume there will be some accountability, I just don't know to whom. The best I can do is assume a sort of global, no, a *universal* humility. Not an angry atheism, or passive agnosticism. Nor cynignosticism, if you will. Cynicism is over-rated, and far too easy. In small doses, cynicism—like irony—provides an essential tempering quality. But to wallow in it, and to dismiss things like hope and faith, is cowardly and un-original. On the other hand, wide-eyed spiritualism doesn't do much good either. Whenever I encounter someone wafting around discovering beauty in all things, I think of Jacob Needleman: "For someone living an uptight, head-restricted experience, a hot bath can feel extraordinary—but it's not a mystical experience. We live such constricted lives that the slightest triggering of a new vital energy gets labeled 'spiritual.'" And so, the best I can offer is an unexciting but honest, "I'm sure there's someone bigger than me in this thing, I just don't know." Call it a spiritual cop-out if you will, but I just want to be on record as saying so. So I can stand there some-day and say, I didn't know what was right, but I never said you were wrong.

That won't get me far with Brother Tim.

I don't remember if anyone stood that night in the granary. It seems no one did, but many years have passed. If they did, they stood late. Brother Tim closed with a prayer. A quiet prayer. Heartfelt. A gentle coda to a fevered symphony. I sat with my head bowed, glad to be where I was. Doubt was still running under the radar. While everyone filed out of the benches, headed for the other end of the granary for chatter and hot chocolate, I sidestepped through the people to the girl with the ringlet. We slipped out a side door. She took my hand and we ran off through the dust devils, down the long dirt track that cut west through the wheat fields. Thunder tumbled around the sky, and skeins of lightning stitched the clouds as the storm hove over us.

The perception of truth evolves through small revelations. Old truths decay in the same way. The revelations are rarely thunderous. They are mites you can barely hear, working be-hind the wood. They are corns of wheat, bits of string. They piggyback our dreams, or wait in the dirt until the day we hit it face-first. We accrete truth like silt. It hones us like wind

over sandstone. Over time, it shifts, regrooves itself, recon-
figures our faith. We are never finished. We are provided
glimpses, if we'll look, but just as quickly, the perspective
shifts, and truth is redrawn at the convergence of a new set of
lines.

Truth does not always strengthen us. False truth yields
false strength, but the truth of clarity cannot be hunted down
or summoned from the heavens. A blinding revelation blinds
more than it reveals.

Beware truth that strikes like lightning.

At a slight rise well beyond the buildings, we stopped to
turn back, and knowing I might never see her again, I gathered her up in my arms. The first fat raindrops were popping
in the dust, and we held each other tight, faces thrown back,
souls wide open to the water and the fire, and the wind sent
Brother Tim's words spinning through the wheat, blowing
them out across Chugwater Flats to mingle with the spent
breath of long-dead buffalo.

1999

Postscript

ABOUT THE PHOTOGRAPHERS

The covers of *Population: 485* and *Off Main Street* are composed on photographs made by John Shimon and Julie Lindemann. I admire the way they work.

○ ○ ○

We met in prison. And that's where the David Allan Coe–Merle Haggard shtick terminates, because John Shimon and Julie Lindemann are photographers, and I am a writer for hire, and we were sent to the Big House under the aegis of a popular magazine. A freelance gig. A single afternoon, in and out. Medium-security, no less.

Still, it was a distinctive introduction——we were, after all, photographing and interviewing lifers, men who had killed other men——and it led to a wind-down in the back room of a small-town tavern. Turned out we were all three products of rural Wisconsin. John's dad raised hogs, Julie's father was a cheese maker. My family milked cows and raised sheep. We talked 4H, FFA and lambing, and parsed the virtues of Holstein production versus Jersey cream. We discussed the desperations and satisfactions of the freelance life.

The shared affinities served as a nice icebreaker, but my interest in Shimon and Lindemann remains sustained because it has given me reason to ponder what it is we are striving at when we tag something—a process, a lifestyle, an art form—with the "alternative" label.

The discipline of photography has a history of serial abandonment. Old technology and process are discarded for new. Inevitably, some visionary Luddite protests, pointing out that "new" is no synonym for "improved." In 1902, the visionary was a man named Alfred Stieglitz, who maintained that the photographic orthodoxy had become stultified by the pursuit of the perfect image. By obsessing over trivial details and compulsively retouching their work, said Stieglitz, mainstream photographers were pandering to mass taste, trading soul for slickness.

Country music fans will recognize the nature of the contention. Reverting to processes that drew on the past and yielded more visual ambiguity, Stieglitz and his group of like-minded contemporaries formed the Photo-Secession movement, eschewing meretricious perfection for a rougher but more compelling look. You might call it "alt-photography."

Shimon and Lindemann are Photo-Secessionist descendants. Their experiments with vintage equipment began in the mid-1980s, and were born, according to Julie, "out of poverty—we couldn't afford new equipment." When we met in early 1999, they had just purchased a circa 1913 12 × 20 Folmer & Schwing banquet camera—essentially, a thirty-pound box of lumber and glass.

The primitive, often cumbersome nature of the equipment, coupled with limitations in depth of field, requires the photographers to slow down, to focus intently on subject and composition. The imperfections and metallic characteristics inherent in "historic" development processes infuse the images with artistic power and substance. Finally, by incorporating elements of modernity (harsh electronic flash, stark urban backdrops), Shimon and Lindemann charge their subjects—elderly artists, small-town strippers, backwater punks and junkies, clean-scrubbed farm kids—with an iconic immediacy, at once timeless and contemporary.

Freewheeling discussion of any "alternative" movement is inevitably gummed up with qualifications, asterisks, and aspersions. Like alt-country, alt-photography spans a spectrum ranging from hard-core purists to outright gimmickry. Some artists—the duo of McDermott & McGough, for instance—remove themselves completely from contemporary life, to a place where flashbulbs are heresy. Others grab a wooden view camera to focus as much attention on themselves as their subjects.

Those of us looking and listening are a skeptical lot. We will not slap the "authentic" label on something just because the artist used vintage tools, be it a Telecaster or an 8 × 10 Deardorff. I like the work of Shimon and Lindemann because I feel they have struck the balance. They respect their audience by respecting their subjects, who, while forced into extended poses out of deference to the archaic nature of the equipment, address the camera full on, often with stark intensity. Whether their subjects are plain or eccentric, strong or down-trodden, you get the sense they are standing there under their own power, in every sense of the phrase. Alternative in their own way, they are a reminder of the well-remarked irony that "alternative" can in fact be euphemistic for "authentic."

In a parallel sense, the most "alternative" element of the Shimon and Lindemann self-portrait, *Re-Ringing the A*, is not that Julie is mechanicking in her black vinyl bra, but that John is truly putting new rings in his grandfather's A-model tractor.

It helps, I think, that Shimon and Lindemann work among their own people. After a valuable postadolescent stretch in dislocation—art school, pink hair, punk band (Hollywood Autopsy), music zine (*Catholic Guilt*), a stretch in New York City's East Village art scene—they have been working out of hometown Manitowoc, Wisconsin, for the past thirteen years. When they pull the black hood over their shoulders and peer into the Folmer & Schwing, the image on the glass is upside down and backward. By now, it just seems natural.

Credits/Permissions

Portions of the introduction previously appeared in *Publisher's Weekly Daily* and on the "Latest News" page of www.sneezingcow.com.

Some of the essays in this collection were drawn from the author's two previous volumes published by Whistlers and Jugglers Press: *Big Rigs, Elvis & the Grand Dragon Wayne* (1999) and *Why They Killed Big Boy . . . and Other Stories* (1996).

Essays in this collection previously appeared in the following publications:

College Lives: An Anthology of Higher Learning (Prentice Hall, 2000): "Scarlet Ribbons."

Hope: "A Way with Wings," "The Fat Man Delivers Christmas" (appeared as "The Bus of Dreams"), "The Roots Remain," "Taking Courage," "Catching at the Hems of Ghosts," and "RSVP to the KKK" (appeared as "Take This Personally").

Men's Health: "Rock Slide!"

No Depression: "Farther Along," "The Road Gang," "End of the Line for a Depot Man," "Clarence 'Gatemouth' Brown" (appeared as "Sittin' on His Dock with the World at Bay"), "Ramblin' Jack Elliott" (appeared as "On the Road"), "Steve Earle: Hard-Core Troubador" (under the byline Michael Ryan), and "About the Photographers" (appeared as "Authentically Alternative").

Orion: "Swelter," "Houses on Hills."

Road King: "Rolling Thunder," "The Haul Road," "Aaron Tippin: A Holler Full of Trucks" (appeared as "Aaron Tippin: A

Workin' Man's Workin' Trucks"), and "Sara Evans" (appeared as "Three Days on the Road with Sara Evans").

Salon.com: "What We Want" (appeared as "Belize in the Dark").

Troika: "The Fat Man Delivers Christmas," "Fear This," and "RSVP to the KKK" (appeared as "RSVP to a Racist").

The Toastmaster: "Hirsute Pursuits" (under the byline Michael Ryan).

Utne Reader: "Fear This" (appeared as "Bumper-Sticker Bravado").

Wisconsin Academy Review: "Manure Is Elemental" (appeared as "Manure Happens").

Wisconsin West: "Life in the Fat Lane" (under the byline Michael Ryan).

The World & I: "Big Things" (early version appeared as "Larger Than Life"), "You Are Here," and "The Osmotic Elvis" (appeared as "The Unshakeable Elvis"). All versions within are reprinted with permission from *The World & I* magazine, a publication of the Washington Times Corporation.

BOOKS BY MICHAEL PERRY

POPULATION: 485
Meeting Your Neighbors One Siren at a Time
ISBN 0-095807-3 (paperback)

The local vigilante is a farmer's wife armed with a pistol and a Bible, the most senior member of the volunteer fire department is a cross-eyed butcher with one kidney and two ex-wives (both of whom work at the only gas station in town), and the back roads are haunted by the ghosts of children and farmers.

"Swells with unadorned heroism. He's the real thing."
—USA Today

OFF MAIN STREET
Barnstormers, Prophets & Gatemouth's Gator
ISBN 0-06-075550-4 (paperback)

Perry serves up a wise and witty collection of essays. This is a diverse yet generous survey of the author's talents as a skilled journalist, penetrating observer, and rural-bred wise man of Wisconsin. His commentaries on everything from truck drivers to country music both enlighten and entertain.

"A sensitive, new-age Hemingway . . ." —Salon.com